The Powerful Radio Workbook:

- *A comprehensive step-by-step guide to show prep and effective aircheck methods that work!*
- *For managers, programmers and talent.*
- *Proven methods to achieve top ratings and great shows.*
- *Techniques to guide programmers and talent to the next level of performance!*

What the industry is saying about CREATING POWERFUL RADIO:

"A tremendous work!"
— Scott Shannon, Program Director, **WPLJ-FM**, New York

"A fine guide for people inside the radio biz and an explanation of that biz to people outside, including the people who would like to get in. It's the kind of book where the reader will often think 'Oh, that's why they do that.'"
— David Hinkley, *New York Daily News*

"This should be required reading in every newsroom and in every radio station."
— *Radio World*

"**Creating Powerful Radio** might eventually make an executive's job at a satellite formatted affiliate much tougher."
— Peter Hunn, *Professor-Communications Studies Department*, State University of New York, Oswego

"One of the best books of its kind."
— Mary June Rose, *Program Director,* **WGN**, Chicago

"Valerie is a big picture thinker. Great insight for the novice as well as tenured professionals."
— David Kantor, President, AMFM Radio Networks and Sr. VP AMFM, Inc./Operations

"Everyone in radio, no make that anyone who communicates for a living should read this."
— Phil Hendrie, *Syndicated air personality,* Premiere Radio

"This is the book I wish someone had given me when I first got into radio."
— David G. Hall, *Program Director,* **KFI**, Los Angeles

"It's great. Read it."
— Kim Komando, *Syndicated Talk Show Host,* WestStar

"Good usable advice."
— Ed Pyle, *Executive News Producer,* **KNX**, Los Angeles

"It's my bible."
— Åsa Paborn, *Executive Producer,* **P3** Swedish Radio

"Brilliant."
— Phil Taylor, **BBC**, Scotland

"My copy keeps getting stolen off my desk."
— Cathy Hughes, *CEO,* Radio One

"We bought copies for the entire staff."
— Viktor Worms, **Antenne Bayern**, Munich

"I carry it around with me."
— Bob Mackowycz, *Program Director,* **CFRB**, Toronto

"**Creating Powerful Radio** contains valuable tips and information geared at presenters, managers and programmers."
— Julia Sullivan, *Music & Media*, UK

"I loved the book. I recommend it to everyone and I use it in my classes."
— Jo Maeder (The Rock 'N Roll Madame), *Air personality and instructor,* New York University

"Packed with insights, it's well written and fun to read. It's obvious why so many radio people consider this a must!"
— John Sawatsky, *Professor of Journalism, Carleton University,* Ottawa

"Useful and practical."
— Jan Ørskov, *Journalist,* Danmarks Radio

"Wonderful."
— Paul Fisher, *Program Director,* **CHFI**, Toronto

The Powerful Radio Workbook

by Valerie Geller

Edited by Turi Ryder

Prep
Performance
Post Production Planning

Airchecking and other methods for developing talent and the programmers who manage them.

M Street Publications
A division of M Street Corporation
54 Music Square East, Suite 201
Nashville, TN 37203
+1-615-251-1525

Library of Congress Cataloging-in-Publication Data

Geller, Valerie

The Powerful Radio Workbook / Valerie Geller

p. cm.

ISBN: 0-9647930-5-9
Library of Congress Catalog Card Number: 99-98007

1. Communications 2. Radio/Television 3. Journalism
4. Broadcast News 5. Media
6. Title

First Printing: 2000

Original cover design by Veikko Anttila, VIL Design, Helsinki, Finland adapted by Janet M. Wocken. Book design by Janet M. Wocken.

Printed in the United States of America

10 9 8 7 6 5 4 3 2 1

The Powerful Radio Workbook

by Valerie Geller
Edited by Turi Ryder

NASHVILLE

Other books by Valerie Geller:

Creating Powerful Radio: A Communicator's Handbook for News, Talk, Information and Personality.

VALERIE GELLER

The Powerful Radio Workbook

Prep
Performance
Post Production Planning

Airchecking and other methods for developing talent and the programmers who manage them.

For Managers, Programmers, and Talent

Edited by Turi Ryder

Acknowledgments

Thank you to Turi Ryder for editing this work and contributing her thoughts, ideas, and broadcast experiences.

Thanks also to Anne Chaabane, Susanne Whatley, Scott Adams, Elizabeth Salazar, Lee Harris, Sean Ross, Elizabeth Dribben, Sheri Inglis, Amalia Gonzalez, David Gleason, Åsa Paborn, Lynn Jimenez, Danny Ortiz, Laurel Ornitz, Melissa McConnell, J. Ruth Gendler, Dana Monosoff, Ron Lando, Alice Lando, Denise Jimenez Adams, and Marie Sandgren for looking over the manuscript and for their ideas, support and editorial suggestions.

My gratitude also to contributors Bobby Ocean (for the cartoons) Jerry Bell, Susan Berkley, Dan Vallie, Bernard Gershon, Mackie Morris, Jaye Albright, Tom Zarecki, Janet Wocken, Jay Severin, Guy Zapoleon, Howard Price, Randy Lane, Andy Beaubien, Denise McIntee, Alan Eisenson, Lorna Ozmon, Deborah Potter, Tommy Kramer, Kelli Grisez, June Barnes, and, of course, to M Street Publishers Pat McCrummen and Robert Unmacht.

Foreword

Just the other day I pulled out a copy of the first American Top 40 with Casey Kasem from July 4, 1970. I like listening to this show every once in a while, because it's a wonderful reminder of why I got into this business in the first place. As a child, I lived each week for American Top 40. I loved the music, but I really wanted to be Casey Kasem. It was that unmistakable voice, those interesting stories about the music, the long-distance dedications—it was a recipe for success that endures to this day.

Kasem provided many of today's broadcasters with the inspiration to get into radio. Great personalities have always played a vital role in helping radio stations achieve the ratings they need to flourish. And, they've also acted as conduits, sparking a passion for radio in those who would dream of sending their own voices over the airwaves.

Today, because of competition from such new media as satellite radio, cable radio and the internet (to name just a few), there's an even greater demand for compelling personalities.

But while demand is high, the business realities of consolidation in the broadcast industry have stunted our ability to nurture and develop truly great talent. Fewer programmers are doing more work than ever, and time is at a premium. Those once-mandatory aircheck sessions are now an endangered species. With Wall Street peering over our collective shoulder, the pressure is on to increase sales. So stations typically hire more salespeople and offer them extensive training. Meanwhile, on the other side of the building, those personalities who are responsible for getting the ratings that boost the sales are offered little, if any, training.

A new generation of broadcasters is manning our radio stations, many of whom have never received proper training themselves. So even if they had the desire and the time, how could today's programmers provide the training and guidance needed to produce exceptional personalities?

In her first book, ***Creating Powerful Radio***, internationally known broadcast consultant Valerie Geller offered us valuable advice about how to find, train and develop talent. Not too long after the book's release, she was hit with the realization: In her quest to cover all the aspects of developing great radio, she'd left one out -- how to aircheck. An oversight? Perhaps. But what she soon realized, as she turned to friends and colleagues for inspiration, was that the art of taking airchecks, dissecting them and using that analysis to help a personality progress from "good" to "great" was, in itself, an untapped area worthy of its own treatment. And so began the months of research and writing that have culminated in the book you now hold, ***The Powerful Radio Workbook***, the Prep, Performance, & Post-Production Planning.

It's a step-by-step guide for program directors (and all radio managers) on how to help develop and manage talent using proper and proven airchecking techniques. Drawing from her own years of experience, as well as the experience and talents of such respected radio consultants as Guy Zapoleon, Randy Lane and Jaye Albright, Geller walks us through all of the key areas. For example, how do you evaluate the reasons why a morning show like Howard Stern's works, but yours doesn't? Geller explains how to identify the generators and reactors in talent that will help you assemble a team that works. From doing show prep to creating powerful promos, from rating job performance to producing the killer aircheck that's going to get you that next job. Geller has done a masterful job of creating an essential guide for radio managers, program directors and talent alike. If, after completing this workbook, talent still isn't living up to their potential, perhaps they should get a new set of liner cards: "Would you like to super-size that?" and "Please drive through!"

—Tony Novia
Contemporary Hit Radio Editor
RADIO & RECORDS

Glossary of Terms

NOTE: *Show Prep, Promo, PD* and *Aircheck* are common usage broadcast terms within the United States. However, if you work outside North America, some of these terms may be new to you. Here are brief definitions of each:

Show Prep: Abbreviation for *show preparation.* Seven days per week, twenty four hours per day, the gathering of thoughts, ideas, materials, articles, experiences for use on the show. Also guest selection, booking of guests.

Promo: Abbreviation for promotional announcements used to let listeners know what is coming up on future shows. The purpose is to create interest and enthusiasm for personalities, news, traffic, weather, songs or other station events.

Aircheck: Noun: Tape of a show used for review purposes.
Verb: A session at which talent works with the tape to improve on-air performance by expanding good habits and elements and eliminating weaker areas.

PD: Abbreviation for program director or program manager--the person in charge of managing, selecting and developing on-air talent.

Formatics: The basic elements required of each host or program to give the station consistency and structure, meet legal requirements and improve ratings. These may include call letters, dial position, time checks, station taglines, and regularly scheduled features, such as contests.

Contents

Contents

Continued

The Powerful Radio Workbook

The Powerful Radio Workbook:

Introduction

Introduction

"You must have chaos within you to give birth to the dancing star."
—Nietzsche

It was disaster. I could not believe it. There I was holding a finished copy of my first book, *Creating Powerful Radio,* in my hands. It should have been a wonderful moment, but *what had happened to the aircheck chapter?* How could an entire chapter be missing? I *knew* it had been sent from my computer to the editor to the publisher, so what had gone wrong? I didn't sleep for a week.

That missing chapter was pivotal. Geared toward helping programmers, it dealt with methods of developing air talent by review and analysis of what they had done. It contained specific ways of listening to a tape of a previous show to help a talent grow to the next level of performance.

M Street publisher Pat McCrummen calmly tried to reassure me that it was going to be OK. Pat has published lots of books and, I imagined, had been through this kind of experience before. "Hey, maybe you'll do another book, an entire book on airchecking," Pat suggested. I gritted my teeth. It was like asking a woman on the delivery table who has just given birth to triplets, "When are you planning to have the next one?" As it turned out, however, Pat was right.

The following month, I worked in Europe. While in Sweden, my next project was cancelled. My client and friend Anne Chaabane suggested, "As long as you have a couple of spare weeks with nothing to do, why not get started on that aircheck workbook?" She offered me her home. I began work on the new book, the next day, at Anne's kitchen table.

This workbook is meant for managers, programmers, and talent. In many radio formats, from music to news and talk, particularly in medium and smaller markets, the PD *is* air talent.

Those who do not have the luxury of a talented or interested coach, programmer, or airchecker, must "self-check." It is usually easier with another person in the room, but, even if you are on your own, this book offers techniques to help you improve your show.

The secret of managing successful radio stations is finding, hiring and then developing good people. Consolidation has left many smaller stations, which at one time served as "farm teams," or training grounds for new people, opting for cheaper syndicated programming instead. There are fewer places where inexperienced but gifted talent can learn how to master their art and grow. This is why airchecking, the fastest and best way to progress, is critical.

Airchecking is considered standard operating procedure in the United States. Much to my dismay, I have found that very few people in Europe aircheck. But now, around the world, the stakes are higher and commercial radio competition is becoming a way of life. The interest in learning specific aircheck methods, tips, and techniques to grow and develop on-air talent has escalated.

This workbook is divided into the following main sections: **Personalities/ Talent, Show Prep,** on-air **Performance** and **Post Production Planning**, the aircheck session. There are also sections on **News** and **Promos.** The worksheets are set up as samples of actual show worksheets.

You will find dozens of "rules" in this book. Remember the most important one: be prepared to break the rules if you come up with a better way to do something.

This material comes from my life and experiences as a consultant, radio programmer, and air personality. It also helps to have sat in the aircheck hotseat.

I have asked some colleagues, associates, and broadcast programmers, whose work I respect, to contribute their ideas. What amazes me is how similar their methodologies are. In fact, much of the material overlaps. All of these experts have helped develop talent with airchecking. None of them would want to work without it.

Within this workbook, there are work pages and exercises to help you with airchecking. You will also find the contact numbers and addresses for the various contributors listed at the end.

Airchecking, correctly executed, works in any format, any language, and any country in the world.

If you would like further information on
Geller Media International™ or the
Creating Powerful Radio™ workshops or
The Producer's Workshop
contact:

Geller Media International
666 West End Avenue
Suite 11-M
New York, NY 10025

phone +1-212-580-3385
fax +1-212-787-6279

email Vgeller@aol.com
internet http://www.gellermedia.com

The Powerful Radio Workbook:

Personalities/ Talent

The Powerful Radio Workbook:

Personalities/ Talent

"The writer is always tricking the reader into listening to his or her dream."
—Joan Didion

"He who hesitates is a damned fool."
—Mae West

Where Do We Find Tomorrow's Talent?

In her Hollywood novel, *Star Country*, Jill Robinson suggests that "star potential," or raw talent, is easy to spot: "Long before the fame hits, the star's the different one. The leader—or the weird one. The motor's there. You want to feed off it; use its heat."

The stars of broadcasting share certain traits. Genuine talent are true individuals, gifted storytellers, and good listeners, as well as articulate communicators. They have original thought, intelligence and passion. These people have a spark of life and a sense of humor. They get a kick out of things. They burn with curiosity. Some have a formal academic education; all have a lot of life experience. These are people who naturally connect with others—individuals with ideas and things to say. They tend to be a little ahead of popular trends. They must be seen and heard.

Developing talent, product and content requires another element: faith. There must be someone on staff—a manager, producer or programmer—who has the ability to find the right people and bring them into the fold. The ability to recognize talent is a talent in itself.

Veteran broadcaster Teddy Fregoso, general manager of XRPS-AM 1090, helped build Spanish radio in Los Angeles, the largest and most diverse Spanish language radio market in the United States. Fregoso's greatest asset is his unparalleled success in judging talent. He has launched the careers of dozens of major radio personalities.

Fregoso understands the universally successful formula for finding powerful air talent: "try them and see if it works." In a January, 1998, interview in the *Los Angeles Times*, Fregoso explained, "The secret to finding talent is simple: give people a chance. How can you tell if you have a good boxer unless you give him some fights?"

Talent is inborn, but broadcasting can be taught. That is why airchecking plays such a fundamental role in developing personalities. When you find people with potential, someone must take the time to develop and coach these individuals in ways that will maximize their skills, not kill them.

Geller Media International broadcast consultant Denise McIntee has years of experience finding and developing new radio talent. Denise advises programmers:

> Be on the lookout for colorful characters in your everyday life. Ask friends, business associates, relatives, and neighbors. Often, they can tell you about an obscure cable-TV host on at 4:30 in the morning who was totally entertaining, or a local stand-up comic who had the patrons in stitches. Teenagers are a valuable resource as well. They hear about the latest trends or hottest acts about a year ahead of everybody else.

Denise McIntee

> Radio stations are loaded with born entertainers, and not just the people on the air. Look closely for the [off-air] employees who are surrounded by staff when they walk in the office. These are the people everyone looks to for entertainment. Their electricity may translate onto the airwaves.

> Sadly, most programmers will not give an audition to anyone without an established track record or who has not honed his or her craft in a smaller market. These programmers lack confidence in their ability to discover a "diamond-in-the-rough."

Give It Time

It is appalling to observe various local stations and networks hire and fire talent in haste if the show is not a "two-book wonder." One of the problems with our industry right now is the complete lack of commitment to talent on the part of management. Remember, it took *60 Minutes* ten years to find its audience.

The original *Star Trek* series was cancelled after just three seasons, because it had "failed." It took reruns for the audience to discover Captain Kirk and Mr. Spock and get hooked on the show. *Star Trek* in television, spin-off shows, movies and books has been breaking records for more than thirty years.

Superstar comedian Jerry Seinfeld exhibits a framed memo from NBC-TV declaring that the initial research on his new situation comedy showed a weak response, a poor supporting cast, and that most viewers who had seen the test pilot would not want to watch it again. The network only ordered four episodes. But somebody had faith in the series, and it paid off.

If producer Garry Marshall hadn't believed in his very funny and talented sister, Penny, and hired her as an actress in his TV sitcoms *Happy Days*, and the *Odd Couple*, TV's long running *LaVerne & Shirley*, as well as the movies *Big, Awakenings,* and *A League of Their Own* might never have been made. Incidentally, talk-host Rosie O'Donnell's talent was initially recognized by Penny Marshall, who believed in her and brought O'Donnell's career along.

Broadcasting is filled with these examples: Talk-show-host Sally Jessy Raphael lost eighteen jobs before she found one that showcased her talent and could grow an audience. The scenario is similar with Oprah Winfrey and dozens of other stars who just needed someone to support and believe in their talent, and enough time for their shows to take off.

Let It Grow

Building an audience for both talent and a format is a process. It's tempting to pull the plug if results are not immediate, but a little patience and consistency can go a long way toward success.

Growing tomatoes takes a certain amount of time. So does digging an oil well. So does building a news/talk radio station. Managers and owners hate to hear this, but in my experience, with very few exceptions, it takes **three years** to build a talk station.

From June, 1988, to June, 1991, KFI-AM in Los Angeles struggled to launch its new talk format. No matter what they did, the ratings barely moved from around a 1.9 to 2.5, similar to what the numbers had been during their last gasp as a music station.

Every single bus board in traffic-infested Southern California was plastered with KFI ads. You could hear the station playing everywhere. People were talking about Rush Limbaugh and the other talent. The *Los Angeles Times* printed six huge cover stories in its entertainment section about the various KFI hosts, but still the numbers hardly budged. Cox Broadcasting stuck with it. They believed in the format. By this time, the company had spent money on programming, talent, promotion, and an award-winning news department, so they hung on without making major changes. After the "three-year build"—success. Today, KFI is one of the most listened-to talk stations in the English-speaking world.

Talent—Be Yourself

It is a good thing to learn from other talent on the air. However, it never really works to become a Xerox of someone else. There are many programmers who look for a Paul Harvey, Howard Stern, or Oprah Winfrey "type." But each of these people made it on unique talent, not by copying others.

Just as vocalists may "try on" characteristics of other musicians during early development, they do not become great until they find their "own" voices. Helping each talent to do that is a large part of the skill of a good program director, manager, consultant, or talent coach.

Managers—Right-casting

A huge part of right-casting is letting your staff know what is expected of them.

Do not expect a serious interviewer or journalist to go on the air in morning drive and be a laugh riot. It is not the nature of that individual's talent. On the other hand, do not get upset if your funny, talented, childlike jokester makes the occasional inappropriate remark. That is what you hired him or her to do.

Right-casting is vital. If you were a movie director, you would not cast Arnold Schwartzenegger in the part of an old, bald, chemistry professor. He could play the part, but he is better playing his "strengths."

So, Who Are These People, Really?

Ask yourself how well you know the employees at your radio station, both the on-air personalities and the support staff. Are you able to perceive their natural talents and abilities? Can you tell what they *might be able to do*, as well as their current capabilities and accomplishments? Do you know what they really hope to achieve at your station?

Before a surgeon operates, he or she performs a thorough examination in order to make an accurate diagnosis. They ask lots of questions. The problem may not actually require surgery. In radio, we sometimes operate without the examination.

On the following pages are some questions I've used to help people decide whether or not they, or members of their staffs, are correctly cast in their current positions. Pay attention to the answers. Look for potential.

Key Questions:

"Sometimes when you are leading [an expedition] you have to say whatever you can to keep people on your side. It doesn't matter if people believe what you say or not. They need to see you believe it. That's what leadership is about."
—Philip Kerr (on mountain climbing)

Passion Quotient

Do you listen to the station on your own time because you like to? Are you proud of your station?

If the answer is yes, you are probably at the right radio station.

If offered your current job again today, what would be something you would ask for other than more money? Why did you want the job you are doing now?

Some may have thought it would be an easy paycheck. Others fought hard for a chance to be on the air. There is a lot of prestige and power that comes with our titles. It sounds good to be able to say, "I am a journalist" or "I run a radio station."

The actual work is another matter. Did you become a program director because you thought that was the next job to take after hosting a talk show? Do you miss being on the air every day? Did you become a general manager because you were offered a promotion and now find yourself in sales meetings when you would much rather be working with talent and marketing?

Are you sick and tired of getting up at 3:00 am, even if you do host the most successful morning show in town? Did you join a team show because you liked working with your co-host but he got fired and you hate his replacement?

Did you become a radio host for the allure it had to the opposite sex? Are you married with a spouse who is threatening to leave if you make one more cross-country move?

Did you go into production because you wanted to write comedy and make clever parody songs but now you have so many spots to create that you never get to produce a single "bit" or creative segment for a show?

Did you think when you started as a journalist that you would be the next Walter Cronkite, and now you host a Hollywood gossip show? Were you planning to be rich and famous?

As the old expression goes, there is nothing as predictable as change. It may be that your job has changed, or that you have.

It is possible that a few modifications in your working life would make your job right for you again. Hire an assistant production director. Get a new co-host. Move to afternoons. Spend time with marketing. It is also possible that you are now incorrectly cast, not because you cannot do your job, but because you do not wish to do it. If you find yourself looking longingly at a position you never thought you would want, ask yourself why it appeals to you.

What is a perfect day at work for you? What is your favorite aspect of the work you do?

That which comes easily to you is probably what you are best at doing. How much of that do you get to do? Do you have many perfect days at work? Is there an opportunity to do more of what appeals to you in your present position? This is an area each host, manager, and programmer should look at from time to time.

How often do you have a great idea for somebody else's show or feature? Do you share it with the talent or keep it to yourself?

If you can pass material along or be of assistance, you are demonstrating courage, leadership, and a generous personality. You have a vision of the total health of the station. You are a team player. This attribute would serve you well either as a manager or as a member of a team show.

TALENT:
Do you feel ruled and restricted by the station's format clock, or do you feel you have enough control and discretion to structure your show according to the needs of the moment?

If you are able to work within the confines of your format, yet have enough leeway to pursue the occasional "magic moment" or news emergency, you are probably working with supportive management. They believe in your ability to discern when something is in the best overall interest of the show and the station. They also are confident you will cover your basic formatic obligations. You have their trust.

MANAGERS:
Are you willing to risk? Do you feel uncomfortable when you hear the format being broken?

If you know that nine times out of ten your format is going "out the window" for a good reason, then you are demonstrating the kind of flexibility that can only come when you have confidence in your air staff.

TALENT:
Do you have total control of your show?

Almost nobody has that, unless you own the station. But, your goal should be to leave the studio each day feeling: "That was me. That was what I wanted to do on the air today." If you finish your show feeling as though you executed somebody else's agenda, with no personal stake in the outcome, you are probably miscast.

MANAGERS:
Do you feel you or your producers are constantly forcing ideas on the talent? Do you feel you must hold the reins tightly to assure that he or she will do a particular type of show every day? Do you feel you are in a wrestling match with the talent for control of the show?

If so, either you are controlling the show out of fear the talent is inept, you are trying to put a square peg in a round hole and the talent is miscast, or you would prefer to do the show yourself.

TALENT:
When it comes to your show, are you more comfortable playing it safe than taking chances on the air? Do you worry about looking foolish?

Superstar performers take a few chances. If they spent a lot of time being anxious about their images, they would miss opportunities to be great. It takes bravery to risk looking silly in front of an audience, but your listeners appreciate courage even if you fail. If the thought of looking undignified petrifies you, perhaps you should try something safer.

When there is a mistake on the air, is it always someone else's fault? Who is to blame for sloppy on-air presentation?

Successful talent take a lot of responsibility for their shows. If something goes wrong on the air, they do not throw up their hands, blame the equipment or the producer, and give up for the rest of the hour. They dump the boring guest, look up an expert's phone number, or carry the microphone down to the street. In short, they are willing to do whatever it takes to achieve a quality air product.

- If the station has no budget for newspapers and magazines, successful talent buy their own.
- If the station cannot afford a piece of equipment, motivated employees go out and find a sponsor who is willing to provide the product on trade.
- An executive producer once organized a collection among the staff to buy a much-needed tape deck.
- A manager went to the pharmacy and bought stomach medication for an ailing newscaster.

A program director once told me, "I'd get down on my knees and shine (the host's) shoes if that would help him do a better show."

In a well-cast broadcasting scenario, if something goes wrong, each person involved, from the program director to the call screener, comes up with an idea of how he or she could help make it better the next time. If you are not willing to take responsibility for your product, ask yourself why you are doing this job.

What makes you angry at work?

Most people get angry at anything they perceive as unfair. Radio is definitely a business in which, as George Orwell says in *Animal Farm,* "some animals are more equal than others." A lot of radio performers are, at least on a local level, "stars." They get treated differently, with a lot of extra privileges. They are stars because of their talent, and talent is not distributed fairly. It takes many people working behind the scenes to support a star. Some people would be better off going for an on-air position in a small market rather than working in an off-air capacity in a large one, because their need to be the star is huge. Others are far happier remaining out of the limelight.

Management can make up for much of the attention that gets directed to the star, but is really owed to the supporting cast, by acknowledging the cast members directly. Still, if you have a chorus line that is miserable not being in the main spotlight, they will be angry, dissatisfied, and do your station very little good. If your background players are envious, believing they should get the same attention as the big on-air attractions, they are miscast.

Radio is a highly demanding business. Often the hours are long and the pay is low. It would be nice if one could staff a station entirely with workaholics, heirs to large fortunes, or those who never need to go home. Although it would be unfair to expect this of any employee, many jobs in broadcasting really do require this. If you enjoy your job, but it never seems to be over, you might find other stations set up their staffs differently, hire more people, and pay them better. It may not be the *type* of work you are doing that is causing you difficulty, but rather *where* you are doing it. In other words, you could be correctly cast doing the same job somewhere else.

Do you believe any of your support people secretly want to be on the air?

Lots of people are drawn to this business and take supporting jobs until the day they can be on the air. Whatever the reasons they took these positions, support people must support their shows. If you are doing your show feeling that the board operator is coveting your job and sabotaging your efforts, this must be fixed. A producer, glaring across the booth and thinking, "I know I could do this show so much better," is not likely to be helping your program.

Although there is nothing wrong with ambition or having long-range broadcast goals, a part of right-casting is knowing the people you hire have the talent and desire to do the job they are currently doing. When they have mastered that position and are eager to move up, managers owe it to them to look at whether or not they would now be well cast in another job. If such a position is not immediately available, tell them. Give them the option, even the assistance, to move to a station where they will be better able to fulfill their goals.

Do you believe the work you do matters?

Having a microphone is not something one should take for granted.

Because aspects of the job can become routine or mundane, it is easy to forget that listeners are giving you their most valuable resource—their time. There is a commitment on the part of the broadcaster to offer information, entertainment, inspiration, or whatever your station has promised to provide.

Do any jobs at the station, other than the one you now have, seem interesting to you?

If they do, why not learn them? There are always vacations, emergencies, and fill-in opportunities. You may find another area of the business that is a better fit for you—one where you would be better cast.

What place does humor have on your show or station?

You might be surprised to find that humor has a place on every radio station. You do not have to be a funny person to have a sense of humor. But it is essential that everyone on the station has an appreciation for the odd, the strange or the quirkier aspects of life.

Moments of levity can be found in topical stories, news, or issues. Even the most serious news programs save a "kicker" for the end of the newscast. If you punish your staff for pointing out the lighter side of a story, you are, in a way, asking them to be other than human.

Can you tell a story three different times in three different ways and keep it entertaining and interesting with each telling?

Because many broadcasters work with subject matter that may not change very much over the course of days, weeks, or even months, they must be able to vary their storytelling. This keeps it interesting to an audience familiar with the material.

It's as if you told your spouse a story. That night you have dinner guests and you tell the story again. The following day, you retell it to a friend over the phone. Your spouse has now heard the story three separate times. However, if you managed to vary your anecdote with different details or a new approach, it was not boring. If you have people on the air who can do this, you have the makings of a great radio station.

What is the best thing about your manager? What is the worst thing about your manager?

If you make an honest inventory of your manager's good and bad qualities, you may find your job is better than you thought it was. What seems like a unsatisfied boss may actually be someone who is working very hard to bring you to the next level of performance. He or she may see potential where you see none. Although you might feel miscast in a certain job, you may be there to learn skills for the next position your supervisor has in mind for you.

Do you feel your manager is the radio police? Can he or she make you do something you don't want to do? Do you work in fear of being caught making a mistake? How afraid are you of getting fired? Does that motivate you?

Everyone has a boss. If you live in fear to the extent that you are not willing to risk management's displeasure, you may be miscast. It is important that you feel strongly enough about your freedom to try new ideas on behalf of your station, your show, or your staff. You must be willing to incur a little fallout once in a while. Sometimes, the powers that be must be obliged, but there should be a little give and take here.

If you are immobilized by fear of losing your job, you should ask yourself the next question:

If you did lose your job, how easily do you think you could find another one?

If the answer is you could not easily replace this job, then you may need to express your creativity in other ways. If you would have to make some sacrifices in the form of a move, pay cut, lifestyle change, etc., and are willing to do so in order to do more creative work that you love, then seeking out a job where you are more properly cast could well be worthwhile.

If you were not doing radio, what work would you do? Is radio the right venue for you?

TALENT:
Does radio fulfill your need to be heard and to express yourself creatively? Does it drain you or energize you to create something new on the air each day? Do you feel satisfied at the end of the day?

Most creative communicators have a lot of artistic abilities. If radio is not the right venue for you, think of some other work that might bc suitable and meet your requirements.

MANAGERS:
Do you feel proud to sell this product? Would you be just as happy selling something more tangible or less controversial?

Many managers would be happy selling or directing in a variety of businesses. If you would be more comfortable managing a different type of company, give yourself permission to move on.

Similar Goals

Part of right-casting is making sure that your goals and the station's objectives work together. Broadcast Programming & Research executive Andy Beaubien, a former program director puts it this way:

> As much as personalities would like to think that their show is their own exclusive artistic responsibility, it is nevertheless part of the station's overall effort. It ultimately must satisfy the station's goals. If the personality's goals and the station's goals are out of sync, the result will be frustration and bitterness on both sides. In almost every case where there is a serious problem between management and an air personality, the underlying cause is usually a conflict between goals or, to put it in the language of the trade publications, 'philosophical differences.'

Talent may also have philosophical differences with the audience. That is fine in many cases, and some talent build careers by flying in the face of convention, but it can be a tough road. Does this mean you should alter your true self to keep your job? McVay Media country music radio programming consultant Jaye Albright speaks from experience when she says:

> As a commercial enterprise, radio does reward the craftspeople who most accurately reflect the current cultural realities. If you can find it within yourself to respect the prevailing value system, while still being true to your own unique creative voice, you may be more successful.

Are You a Generator or a Reactor?

From my experience, I have observed that talent usually falls into one of two categories, *generators* and *reactors*.

In order to coach talent effectively, it helps to identify the talent's strengths and natural abilities. Vallie-Richards Consulting president Dan Vallie suggests; "clearly define the talent's roles. There must be an anchor or director, a creative chief, a producer, etc." Knowing thc type of performer you are working with lets you guide him or her toward his or her maximum performance. The programmer is then able to design powerful radio by making the shoe fit the foot, instead of trying to do it the other way around.

What Is a Generator?

The natural skills of the generator mean that he or she can easily work alone or as part of a team. A generative talent visualizes original ideas. A generator has a strong independent imagination. The generator comes up with a myriad of topics, undaunted by the blank page.

What Is a Reactor?

Reactors are also creative individuals. A reactive talent takes existing ideas and comes up with numerous ways to make them better or more workable.

No less talented than a generator, the reactor nonetheless has a very different style. A reactor alone faces the blank page with terror. However, the moment a reactor comes in contact with a generator, he or she can instantly and very cleverly pick up on remarks, comments, or nuances and be very funny.

A reactor is usually the one who responds to just about any stimulus with an insightful or witty remark. Reactors can have a lot of fun talking back to their TV sets and radios. Reactors work best with other people in the room to spark their creative energy.

Both types of talent are valuable and good, but right-casting here is the key. Forcing a reactor to carry the show as a generator doesn't work, and forcing a strong generator into an equal or subordinate partnership with another talent can lead to an almost painful on-air clash. As a coach, it is your job to identify each person's specific strengths and then to encourage each one to develop those strengths.

Putting two generators together as co-hosts or as a team can sometimes be a disaster. They tend to battle for the microphone, seldom listen to each other, and compete for attention. The show sounds like two kids fighting at the dinner table. It is hard to listen for very long.

Putting two reactors together is not much better. The audience hears them casting a net for ideas over and over again. The process is dull, and, if nothing swims into the net, the show becomes weak and boring.

Electric connection with the audience happens when you have a balance of both elements.

How Do You Tell the Difference Between a Reactor and a Generator?

It is fairly simple. Generators have a lot of ideas and energy. They take huge risks and worry about it later. They have moments of brilliance. They sit alone in a room, and their minds overflow with ideas.

That is not to say that every idea a generator produces is a perfectly conceived show, but they seem to be practically exploding with new material.

If you are looking at a reactive talent, you will notice that he or she is quick with a story, a memory, an imitation or a line for any topic you could give him or her. But you must lead the reactor by giving that first push, that suggestion, or a good opening. Leave the reactor alone in a room with no external catalyst for the show, and he or she is miserable. Reactors may do brilliant interviews, or pick things out of the newspaper that are unique, but they need some kind of initial stimulus to begin the process.

You probably have a reactor on the air if he or she is dull until the news person shows up.

Generators are scarce. Most people are reactors. It is a little like being left- or right-handed. One is no better than the other. If absolutely necessary, right-handed people can be forced to use their left hands, and vice versa. You can certainly force people to improve in the area where they are weaker, but in most circumstances, it is best for the station to take advantage of their natural inclinations.

A Cast of Dozens

You might think it takes a generator to host a morning show. That is not always the case. One reactor, "Casey," found a cast of generators in his listening audience.

"Rita" owned and operated a local beauty salon. She was also Casey's loyal fan and listener. Rita started calling in on a semi-regular basis to chat about hot movies and goings on around town. She was funny and charming and had unique views. Rita became a regular on the show. The listeners started calling in wanting to meet Rita. She participated at station events and appearances.

Next, Casey added another regular listener, a talkative cab driver. Then he found a local construction guy with fix-it tips, who also happened to be single, twenty-eight years old, dating regularly, and happy to talk about his adventures.

Casey continues to add appropriate players as they appear. He has a hot show now with lots of generators to show off his reactive talents. He assembled his own generator-reactor team.

Once you know who your generators and reactors are, you are ready to begin the Prep.

Talent Notes:

Talent Notes:

The Powerful Radio Workbook:

Show Prep

The Powerful Radio Workbook:

Show Prep

"Men are born with two eyes, but with just a single tongue, in order that they should see twice as much as they say."
—Charles Caleb Colton

Why Is Prep Crucial?

A general would never go into battle without a plan. A surgeon would never go into the operating room without a preliminary work-up. Yet it is surprising how many air personalities show up for work and just wait to see what happens. Some days they might get lucky, but for winning over the long haul, show prep is essential. If a talent is prepared, it does not matter if he or she slides in a minute before airtime. The prepared host can still do a great show.

It is *never* an accident when a show is number one. It takes very hard work. The best personalities compile a stack of material from various sources: articles from magazines or newspapers, written ideas, and material collected from the internet.

When I worked with syndicated-host Rush Limbaugh at WABC, I knew I was watching a master of show prep. Rush came in hours before his show.

He didn't go on the air until he'd gone through dozens of newspapers, discussed ideas with his producer, and spent time on the phone talking with anyone from disc jockeys to political leaders. Rush had concepts and stories, but no guests. He found things that interested him, collected them, and shared them with his audience. No one made him do this. Rush did it on his own, because he wanted his show to succeed. He realized the value of show prep.

Everyone has his or her own way of organizing show prep materials, but if a host sounds consistently disorganized on the air, try coming up with another system. If a host is prepared but cannot access an item during the on-air performance, all that prep is wasted and the show will wander.

Some talent are fortunate enough to have trustworthy people, usually producers, who do their show prep and planning for them. It then becomes the talent's job to creatively execute someone else's plan. Nevertheless, a plan still exists.

Creative talent, twenty-four hours a day, seven days a week, are engaged in show prep. Everything in their lives—what they read, eat, feel, experience and even dream—all goes into their shows. Good talent utilize *everything* including their personal experiences and relationships.

How personal can it get? With some air personalities, the best you can hope for in terms of confidentiality is that your name stays out of it. Managers beware: your meetings or conversations with talent could become material.

There *is* a difference between personal and private. No one should be allowed to endanger others or personally harm them in any way. Not only can there be legal consequences to giving specific information about peoples' private lives, but there can be security issues as well. When in doubt, try asking: will the story of the car with the Picasso in the back seat be as compelling if I don't give the car's make and model? Oftentimes a little camouflage enables more creative and dramatic story-telling without risking someone's physical well-being or emotional embarrassment. What is your point? If entertaining your audience is the goal, then does it really matter if something happened to your wife or to "a woman I know...?" Try television's *Dragnet* approach: "The story you are about to hear is true, but the names have been changed to protect the innocent."

Using Humor

Some people are funny; others may not be funny but have great senses of humor. There are those who are hilarious in private, but are not able to access those parts of their personalities on the air.

You can do show prep that improves your ability to be funny on the air. For example, you can learn to become a better storyteller. McVay Media consultant Jaye Albright offers this advice to those who would like to grow and develop in this area, "Read every book in the library about humor. If possible, attend improvisation workshops. These can be mind-expanding releases of creative expression. [When telling a story] memorize specific and colorful details. There is nothing funny about the abstract—comedy emerges from specifics. Make note of them and use them; allow the child who lives within you to emerge. Tell your truth."

Rules for Powerful Prep

"Use everything in your life to create your art."
—Stanislavsky

Here are some ideas and questions to look at when doing show prep.

1) Go With the Moment

Also known as the rule of "out the window."

If something spontaneous happens on the air that is better than what you have prepared, go with it! You would happily take a "side trip" to see the Grand Canyon while traveling through Arizona. The magic moments on radio—a breaking news story or a fabulous caller—happen when you least expect them, and when they occur it is wonderful. Although there is no substitute for walking into the station thoroughly prepared, you must also be willing to throw that stack of stuff "out the window" when something irresistible turns up.

2) Why Are We Doing This?

Always have a specific reason for wanting a guest.
Avoid "guest-o-mania." If a guest has been booked for you, know the reason. Ask the producer, "What has this person done? Why is he or she special?"

Ask: "Will we enjoy this guest even if we are not familiar with his or her latest book or area of expertise?" Think twice before you take the easy way out and book a guest to fill an hour of airtime.

If you have always wanted to meet someone, and he or she lives in your town or is coming to your area, it is perfectly acceptable to invite that person to be a guest on your show, providing that the goal remains to entertain or inform your audience.

Never promise a guest an hour. Instead, ask for a few minutes of his or her time. Make it clear that because this is live radio, it is always possible that a guest may be pre-empted by a breaking story. You have now protected yourself, from the potentially embarrassing situation of having to dump a guest if he or she is boring or if a bigger opportunity arises.

I am frequently asked for a rule about guests. Unless you are doing an interview-based show, I advise using guests as *spice*. Like great seasoning in a bland meal, guests can be wonderful. Good guests can make a show, but they must be gifted communicators with passion and something relevant to say. The best guests are people who have personal experience, with a story to tell, rather than being just experts in their fields.

A guest can also serve as an unwitting foil for savvy hosts with barbed tongues. "John and Ken" in Los Angeles are famous for finding "village idiots" and using them on the air for comedic purposes.

Warning to Managers:

Managers, particularly those oriented to finance, like to hear guests on the air. It demonstrates that the host and producer have done some work to book the show and justify their salaries. They like to see bodies at desks for eight hours a day. Sales reps are asked to turn in lists of people they have called on, called back, or visited. Managers feel comfortable seeing people working. It's that "all in their places with bright shiny faces" song we learned in elementary school. We are accustomed to believing what we see. Management have a hard time accepting that a talent fighting with his or her auto mechanic is actually doing show prep, but it can be true.

Broadcasting is not school, or a factory job where we punch in our eight hours a day. Radio work is different, more like art than manufacturing. A gallery owner would not call an artist at 8:45 in the morning and ask, "Are you at your easel yet? How many brushes have you used?"

The only hard rule for powerful radio is: be prepared and on time for your show. What listeners respond to is the finished product. Our product is on the radio. Our preparation is real but often invisible.

3) Be Prepared

Carry a tape recorder or note pad at all times. Don't forget spare batteries for that tape recorder. If we were working as photographers, we would always have a camera ready. But we work in *radio* and our platform is *sound.* When was the last time you thought to yourself, "I wish I had a tape recorder right now?" They are small and inexpensive. Get one. Carry it. If you are not comfortable carrying a tape recorder, at least keep paper and pen handy so that you can jot down a great idea before it is gone. Great ideas come in the shower; the car; wake you up at night. Write them down.

4) **Make Friends Outside the Business**

Spend time with normal people. If you only associate with journalists and broadcasters, you limit your vision. Expand your horizons. Talk to everyone. Your inner circle should contain people who work outside of radio and have a variety of interests and experiences. Listen to them. Find out what they are thinking, worrying, and talking about. It will help your show tremendously. Read everything. Watch everything. Find mentors. As consultant Randy Lane says: "Hang out with creative people, and learn from them. Study creative performers outside of radio."

5) **Know Your Target**

Know your audience. Do the listeners have a lifestyle that is different than the host's? Probably so. Perhaps a host lives in a busy urban center, whereas the bulk of the station's listeners are suburbanites. You need to know what goes on where they live, too. Read the local press. Drive around to get a feeling for your area. Attend neighborhood functions. Meet people. Get to know your city.

Unless you are Robin Leach, this is not *Lifestyles of the Rich and Famous*. Even if you do not frequent your local Target, K-Mart, or Home Depot, you should at least know people who do. Eat where your listeners eat; shop where they shop. Stay curious, alive, and interested. Check out the internet.

6) **Take a Test Drive**

Discuss show ideas with somebody else. Prep is much easier when you have the luxury of working with a talented producer. He or she can help form questions you will ask on-air and points you will make to engage your audience. Try bouncing the ideas off people around you: the call screener, the PD, the news person, or the station's security guard. It may help you focus on what is really interesting about the topic, or take it in a different direction.

Prep Warning:
Do *not* do your show before the show. Testing out an idea should not be confused with rehearsing a monologue. Save your actual performance for the live microphone. It won't sound as good or as natural the second time around.

7) Pre-produce
Prepare the soundtrack for your show. Any bits, music, etc. that you think you might want to use should be close at hand. Inform your engineer or board operator well in advance if you will require any special technical assistance or equipment. Make sure your equipment is working.

8) Double Check
Before you go on-air with a topic ask:
Is it relevant?
Does it matter?
Do you care?
Do your listeners care?
What will I do if this topic gets boring?
Do I have a fall-back plan?

9) Be Generous
If you have found a topic that would be perfect for somebody else at the station, pass it along. Leave the article, book, note, etc. in that person's mailbox, or give him or her a call or e-mail. The success of the station depends on the efforts of all its creative members.

10) Experiment

Break rules if you can come up with a more successful method. Take what works for you, and leave the rest.

WILL YOU QUIT SAYING, "I DON'T GET IT" AFTER EVERY JOKE

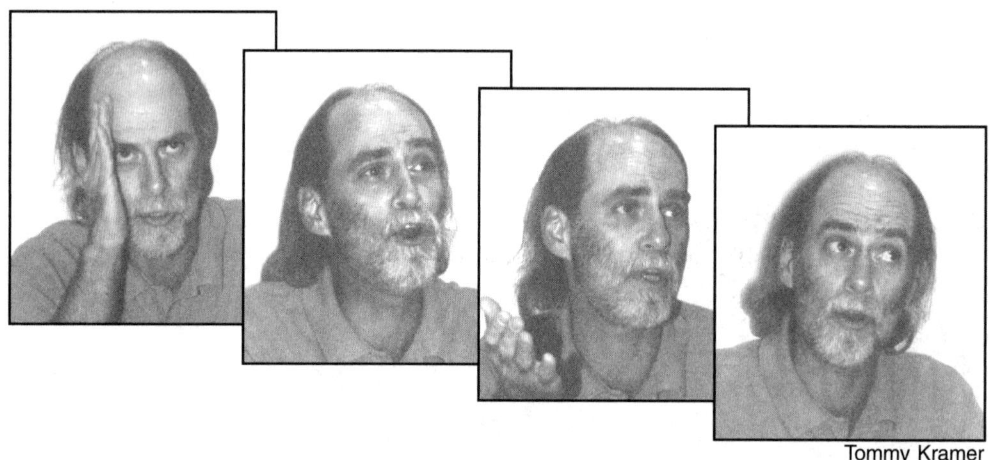
Tommy Kramer

Talc of Total Show Prep

Former air personality and program director Tommy Kramer currently coaches talent for Clear Channel in Dallas. His "tale of total show prep" illustrates what can happen when you do not do your homework thoroughly:

> A talent called with a problem: he had overslept on Tuesday, had no time for show prep and just barely made it in time for his morning-drive show. Yet he and his partner had a great show that day. The next day, the talent did two hours of show prep and arrived on time, but the show was difficult and out of synch. His question for me was "Do I really need show prep?"
>
> This guy got lucky on Tuesday. His creative side bailed him out. But it won't and cannot every day. Wednesday he did tons of prep, but all the work was informational. He had lots of things on tap, but had not thought about where to go with them.
>
> The answer is "yes, you need to do your show prep. But look for balance and prep your creative as well as your informational side."

Prep and Topic Selection

Broadcasters organize their show prep in different ways. There is no "right way," just the way that works for you.

The following examples come from air personality Jay Severin. His sources include newspapers, magazine articles, the internet, plus stories and conversations from his own life. From this prep work, Jay gets three talkable topics/ engaging questions he will use on the air.

Many hosts and producers find it useful to attach the source materials to show prep sheets. For this show, the host would have two newpaper articles plus stories printed from the internet (or data which can be made available on-screen during the show.) Show prep worksheets we use appear as follows:

Topic #1
Source: ***New York Times* article**

Talkable topic or engaging question: date rape vs. "fake" date rape. On college campuses in the area, there has been a rash of alleged date rapes. Some are real, but some may not be. What constitutes "date rape?" Isn't it just rape?

Possible Guest(s): Jay plans to do an open-hour phone opinion discussion.

Here is Jay's actual show open:

> Date rape doesn't exist. There is no such thing as date rape any more than there is such a thing as date murder or date arson or

date bank robbery. There is rape. A vile crime. Then there is seduction. That we now confuse the two is very scary.

Seduction is a completely wonderful natural male skill that we are born and raised to study and perfect every day. It is my job as a boy to do and say and manipulate anything at my disposal in order to get a girl's knickers off. I may lie, promise, cajole, entice; I may use every trick in the book (and my book looks a lot like a set of encyclopedias...). Anything I can do to get a girl to have sex with me is fair as long as I do not use force.

If what we now stupidly call date rape is in fact a real crime, you are listening now to America's biggest serial date rapist.

Topic # 2
Source: ***New York Post, People Magazine*** articles (one on medical ethics, the other detailing the lawsuit).

Talkable topic or engaging question: Should dead people have children? It's now medically possible, but is it right?

A 34-year-old woman's husband was killed in an accident. There is a new medical procedure to harvest sperm from the body of the deceased and implant the still living sperm into the womb of the widow. She wants very much to conceive a child. His family does not want her to do this.

Possible Guests:

- A member of the woman's deceased husband's family.
- A doctor who performs such procedures.
- The lawyer handling this case.

Open-phone/opinion discussion.

Topic #3
Source: Host personal experience plus additional internet data.
Talkable topic or engaging question: Headline story about the New York $70 million lottery.

Jay plans to broaden and develop this topic into three areas.

1) How would $70 million change your life?
2) What subjects of conversation draw total strangers together?
3) If a man won the money, would he be more likely to spend it than a woman? Are there differences in the ways men and women spend money?

Possible Guests: Lottery winners who've spent it foolishly. Psychologist discussing "found money" dynamics.

Open-phone/opinion discussion.

Here is what went on the air:

Tonight they draw the winning ticket. I usually don't buy lottery tickets, but I sure did today. Did you?

There were five or six of us in the men's locker room at the gym this morning. We don't know each other by name. We nod, say "hi" once in a while when we see each other, but we have never had any conversation. All of a sudden, someone off-handedly says, "I guess this is my last workout here, I'll see you guys!" Everybody looks at him. One guys smiles and says "You mean because you're going to win the lottery right?" Everyone laughs and starts yelling: "No way! I've got the winning ticket!" "No I do!"

Then someone says quietly, "Boy that would be great. I've got two kids going to college this fall." Suddenly these men, none of whom had spoken to each other and who probably have very little in common, had found something. Everybody stopped lacing up his sneakers and started talking, fantasizing about winning 70-million bucks. And the amazing thing is that everybody had thought about it before they got to the gym—about how it would change their lives. Do women dream about this?

As for me, I fantasize and I think about buying things, giving money to my family and friends, but mostly I use it as a reality check. I ask myself, what would I really do differently if I won that money. And you know what? The answer is, I'd be right here tomorrow. How about you?

[Break for commercial]

Dig Deep for Talkable Topics/Engaging Questions

None of these ideas was a front page story. Remember to look beyond page one. Take notes from conversations you've had or overheard. Try to come up with at least one story or observation from your own life for each show.

Show Prep/Topic Sources

Worksheet

Articles, news stories etc.

1) What is the **TALKABLE TOPIC**?

2) What is the **SOURCE**?

3) What is the **ENGAGING QUESTION/STATEMENT**?

4) Who is/are the **POSSIBLE GUEST(S)**?

Show Prep/Topic Sources

worksheet

TALKABLE TOPIC # 1: ______________________________

____

____

____

____

SOURCE: ______________________________

____

____

ENGAGING QUESTION/STATEMENT: ______________________________

____

____

____

POSSIBLE GUEST(S): ______________________________

____

____

____

Show Prep/Topic Sources

Worksheet

TALKABLE TOPIC # 2: ______________________________

____

____

____

____

SOURCE: ______________________________

____

____

ENGAGING QUESTION/STATEMENT: ______________________________

____

____

____

POSSIBLE GUEST(S): ______________________________

____

____

____

Show Prep/Topic Sources

Other print items:

1) ____________________

2) ____________________

3) ____________________

4) ____________________

Internet and other information:

1) ____________________

2) ____________________

3) ____________________

4) ____________________

Real-life story: ____________________

____

____

____

____

____

worksheet

Show Prep/Topic Focus

Talkable Radio Topics:

What affects people about this story today?
Pick out the most interesting thing about this subject:

- **WHO:** Who is involved in the story—and of most interest in this story? *Actor Tom Cruise breaks leg.*
- **WHAT:** What happened? Is this the story itself?
- **WHEN:** Is time important here? *April 15th tax deadline; kidnapper will execute the hostage at noon.*
- **WHERE:** Did the story's location matter the most? *A truck accident at Highway 15 has traffic blocked for miles.*
- **WHY:** Look at why things occur. Is why the most interesting part of the story? *Is lack of road/highway funding the reason the bridge collapsed?*
- **HOW:** Does it affect the listener? *HOW much does it cost, HOW does it affect the homeless?*

Now circle the one area of most powerful interest to you. Then circle the one you think is most important to the audience. Emphasize either of these in your opening remarks. Make sure you give both areas lots of attention. Then in order of importance, number the remaining focus points and do your set up.

Show Prep/Topic Focus *(continued)*

worksheet

Topic Prep Sheet:

1) **WHO IS INVOLVED?**______________________________

____

2) **WHAT HAPPENED?** ______________________________

____

3) **WHEN DID IT HAPPEN?**___________________________

____

4) **WHERE DID IT HAPPEN?** __________________________

____

5) **WHY DID IT HAPPEN?**____________________________

____

6) **HOW DID IT HAPPEN?** ___________________________

____

More Prep Methods

Basic preparation techniques are similar for every format. The actual protocol works as well for music as it does for talk radio. Andy Beaubien has programmed many of America's top-rated Album Rock music stations, including WCOZ/Boston; KNX-FM/Los Angeles; KLOL/Houston; and WCXR/Washington, D.C. Andy now heads Broadcast Programming & Research's European offices, based in France. Andy, along with fellow BP&R consultant Jeremy Millar, outlined this method for prepping and running a well-organized show.

Andy Beaubien

Here are Andy's tips on preparing a music show:

Show prep is usually a team effort and not a task assigned to just one person. In most cases, the program producer becomes the official collector of show-prep material, since he or she is often more objective than the show's anchor.

Review

Ideally, show prep begins with a review [aircheck session] of the previous program. This is often accomplished at the daily meeting with the PD. Decide which segments worked and which did not.

Update

The producer updates the team on new material that has arrived. This may include items from publications, syndicated-radio services, press releases, the internet, and so on. The update should include a briefing on the latest news items that may fit the show. The availability of in-studio [or phone] guests should also be reviewed and the producer should be prepared to provide background information on them. It is also good to look at major news, sports, and show-business events which may be upcoming.

Sources

With the overflow of material available elsewhere, the local newspaper need only play a modest role in your show. If you find you are depending on the newspaper for most of your topics, try a "newspaper-free" week.

Some teams hire writers who will generate exclusive material for their shows. You can often find talented free-lance writers who will regularly deliver fully written, customized material for a surprisingly nominal fee.

Topics

Decide on a list of topics for the day's program, and assign a priority to each item. Gather additional information about items that caught your attention. Often you may find that a topic which originally sounded interesting turns out to be a dead-end street. On the other hand, research may uncover amazing facts about a subject that had seemed limited.

If script-writing or pre-recorded material is necessary, the producer can assign these tasks to others on the team. Most talents prefer an outline to a written script, so they can deliver material in their own style.

Production

Pre-recorded material may include interviews with guests not available at airtime, on-the-street interviews, musical excerpts, sound effects, novelty voices, feature intros and outros, and highlights from previous programs.

Schedule

Schedule the program elements on paper. Make sure everyone involved gets a copy. Each program should be planned in quarter-hour segments (or smaller if necessary). Interview guests are also placed on the schedule at this time. The program schedule should be maintained on a daily and weekly basis. A good producer should always have a contingency plan, as last minute guest cancellations are common.

Archives

An essential part of show prep is the maintenance of complete and accurate files. This library should include the following:

- A file of previous daily program schedules
- Copies of scripts and program ideas
- Background material by subject
- Audio files including full-length DAT or videotapes of previous programs and edited program excerpts

> Accurate records allow the team to recycle successful program features. Great guests and new show topics are not always available. A good library will keep the show afloat through slow periods.

Tommy Kramer points out that another, nearly effortless way a team show continues to prep outside the station is to "communicate with each other off the air. An advance phone call or e-mail can prepare your partner or producer for a bit you want to do tomorrow. It gives the other person time to turn it over to his or her subconscious and think of creative ways to contribute. Time spent going to lunch or a ball game together can teach you things about each other's speech patterns, outside interests, etc. that could otherwise take months to learn."

Be Selective

Jaye Albright

It is great when you have ten fabulous ideas for a show, but only need four. But how do you know which topics should make it to the air?

Is there a set criteria for topic selection?

McVay Media consultant Jaye Albright says it very well: "Do something that has something to do with me and my life. It can't be a cliche. It must be original and specific. If it is something from your life, I hope that it becomes a metaphor for something about mine. Something that moves me emotionally, touches me personally, yet is delivered with spontaneity and the knowledge that my time is important. The less it has to do with me, the briefer or the more moving it must be."

Howard Price

There are some guidelines to help you pick topics for stories, talk shows, and bits. WABC TV's Howard Price has had many years of radio experience. The reason Howard has been so successful choosing topics for top-rated *Eyewitness News* in New York, where he is assignment editor, is that he knows how to spot popular issues and trends. He stays ahead of the curve, using these criteria for topic selection:

Your audience is growing more vocal about what they perceive as sameness up and down the dial. They are searching for a sound that reflects their lifestyles and personalities. So remember:

- *You work for "WIFM"*—"What's in it for me?"—and the "me" means your listeners.

- *Every day ask:* What are people really doing? What are they talking about right now at their desks or on the checkout line? How can my program engage in and advance the discussion? Explore problems *and* solutions. Unite your listeners with stories of personal crises or extreme viewpoints.

- *Have the vision and vigilance* to spot trends, take risks, exploit opportunities. Do one thing, or a small collection of things, better, faster, and more reliably than any of your competitors. That is what builds your image in the minds of your listeners.

- *When selecting topics ask:* Will people expect us to cover this? If your listeners know that you can be counted on for great coverage of sports, health, or politics, then they tune to you for those things.

- *People care about things that are close to them physically, emotionally, spiritually or intellectually.* They care about the security of their jobs, the education of their kids, the health of their parents, the cost of their homes, their favorite celebrities, etc. They care about the consequences of the decisions their leaders make. They want the answer to the question, "What does this mean to *me*?"

- *Use radio's immediacy.* Radio can still get more places faster than TV. Do as much live as you can. If there is a current event where you can get a direct call through to the people involved, while TV is still trying to push their camera in someone's front door, radio has the advantage. Pick that topic. Everyone has a telephone in the house, but hardly anyone has a satellite hookup in the living room.

- *Use the news.* Scan the wires, newspapers, magazines, newsletters, on-line services, and the internet for stories that sadden, outrage, inform, enlighten, amuse, or frustrate.

- *Have a friend who has a friend.* Always get a phone number. Keep your rolodex updated. Hang on to phone numbers of all sources. Take advantage of all the sources that offer free directories (the government, universities, TV and radio stations, public relations firms etc). Keep "hot lists" of relevant phone numbers. Today's guests may be tomorrow's sources. Ask them to call you when things are happening.

- *Get a life.* There really is more to life than news, weather, and sports. Explore a broad spectrum of interests. Become a dabbler who knows a little about a lot of things. Be as worldly as your guests and listeners!

- *People want more than just the facts*—they want to understand *why* something is happening.

There is also a basic philosophy behind choosing air talent who can spot a good topic. Alan Eisenson, with whom I have worked over the years, is the program director of WEVD talk radio in New York. At his last position as program director of KXNT in Las Vegas, we took a virtually nonexistent radio station and, through airchecking, created a winner.

Alan Eisenson

Alan says "*Topic selection* is the issue a host chooses to talk about during the show. *Content execution* is how that host takes the issue and makes it into a talkable topic." Alan on choosing topics:

Topic Selection

> The deepest I ever get into content is when I think a host is doing the same topic too often or if I think a host has missed a major top-of-mind issue. Beyond that, I stay out of it. I have found it can harm true talent if you "micro-manage" them. (Of course, I suggest topics all the time, but they are only suggestions.)

When you first hire a talk talent, you should set the overall criteria for content on your radio station. My criteria is that the shows should hold up a mirror and reflect life.

Keeping the target demo in mind, topics should include a wide range of issues. News and politics (local, national, and international), should be there, also general life, pop culture, relationship issues, sports, etc. Hosts should also be able to cull material and stories from their personal lives and translate them into relatable talk shows. Self-disclosure is very important. Anything that affects your life should be covered on your talk show.

Do Not Stifle the Creative Process

My approach to content is that it is not the program director's role to take authority over topics. I never mandate a topic, and I never veto a topic. It is vitally important that the content of a show be solely up to the talk-show host. The host is the one who has to engage the audience, so the topics have to come from his or her gut. His or her opinions and passions cannot be dictated by a program director, general manager, client, or consultant. The host is the artist; the airtime is his or her canvas. Do not take the brush from the artist's hand.

Content Execution

I believe that, as a program director, you must hire talent you can count on to pick topics based on your criteria. You expect them to be creative, interesting, original, have a sense of humor, and be relatable. They should be interested in a wide variety of things, have strong opinions, a deep knowledge base, be articulate, paint pictures with words, really live life, do incisive interviews, make people think, make people laugh, and act appropriately in a variety of prickly situations. If you do not have that trust from the outset, you have hired the wrong talk-show host.

If you truly demonstrate that you trust your talk talents with their own content and you do not interfere with their creative processes, the faster they will trust, respect, and respond to you when you direct and guide them in aircheck sessions.

Brainstorming or the "Collective Creative Process"

"All truly wise thoughts have been thought already thousands of times; but to make them truly ours, we must think them over again honestly, until they take root in our personal experience."
—Goethe

Ideas

It is one of those slow days. You find yourself looking through last Thursday's newspaper for show ideas. What can you do? Try going *inside* the radio station, as well as your own life and experiences.

Do not underestimate the value of living in the world as a source of show prep. Jaye Albright embraces this idea as well:

> "Communication is more about listening and observing your target listener than it is about talking. Live a life. Build off-air relationships. Learn to expose your true feelings. Be vulnerable. Explore your own beliefs. Listen to others talk about their values and beliefs. Open a window to the inner workings of varying points of view. Experiment with safely expressing these differing points of view and then listen to what happens."

Exercise

Imagine that the "price of admission" for every employee at your station each day is to bring in one idea. They wouldn't necessarily have to be good ideas, just something someone noticed, thought about or even experienced in the past twenty-four hours. All the ideas would be written down and go into a fishbowl on the front desk.

Later, at the news, programming, or promotion meeting, the ideas could be poured out on the table and discussed. Not all of the ideas would be good ones. Some might be truly awful. But if one or two were usable, you would be ahead.

Here is one real life example of how a brainstorming process turned into usable prep material for broadcast:

A piece of paper read: *"Last weekend we didn't do anything but paint our house."*

Talent: "Somebody painted their house?"

Producer: "That's all they did?"

Newsperson: "Well, we did. It was about time. We bought the paint two years ago and it's been sitting in the garage since then."

Producer: "I wanted to paint some furniture, but that stuff makes my head spin. At least you were outside."

Newsperson: "It didn't help. I felt sick anyway."

Newswriter: "What kind of paint were you using?"

Newsperson: "Oh, some cheap brand that went on sale right after Christmas."

Producer: "You know, I remember there was some kind of paint they took off the market a couple of years ago. It was supposed to be really toxic. People got sick."

Newswriter: "I wonder what happened to all the paint? If people bought that stuff on sale, stored it, or are still using it, that could be a story."

Suddenly a slip of paper turns into a story, topic, or feature for the radio station. It's original. No other media will have it, because it came from the station's collective creative process.

Andy Beaubien adds his thoughts about the collective creative process:

- Allow for a free interchange of ideas.
- Adopt the principle that there are no bad ideas.
- Make lists and lots of them.
- Postpone decision-making until all of the possible options have been considered.
- Remember that creativity flourishes best in an open and informal atmosphere.

Prep—The Method:

"The very simplest words must be enough. When I say what things are like, everyone's heart must be torn to shreds."
—Bertolt Brecht

How to Master the Art of "Descriptive Detail"—Watch, Listen and Absorb

It is the small, specific details that make a story or image come alive. Little things illustrate, add color, and jazz up story-telling on the radio. Describing a situation, a place, or anything you are talking about will cement an image or create a photo in the listener's mind.

How can you improve your use of detail? Observe everything. Use your own unique thoughts and vision to enhance storytelling. Poets and songwriters work hard to develop this method of spare imagery. It shows you the scene and "takes you there."

Take the example of Bob Dylan's "Mr. Tambourine Man" describing somebody celebrating in the night: *"To dance beneath a diamond sky with one hand waving free..."*

Try using just enough spare and powerful detail so that the listener can see, taste, smell and hear the experience you are trying to communicate. Do this on the radio. Soon it grows easy, even fun, allowing you to put your individual stamp on your observations of life. Filter those through your very own creative process.

Begin by seasoning your everyday off-air conversations with descriptive details. Use all the colors in your verbal paintbox. Make observations of little things in life a part of your normal speech. This way it becomes habit and will come more naturally to you on the air. Get out to places where you have a lot of interesting things to see. Find new places—where you will experience things to talk about on the radio.

Descriptive Detail
Exercise #1

If you can stand looking a bit foolish, and are willing to practice, here is an exercse to help you improve your ability to describe specific details.

Goal of This Exercise

- To describe any event in terms so loaded with sensory information that the audience actually feels transported.
- To build and stockpile files of mental images you can immediately call up when you are on the air.

Exercise

(Do this alone—with no one watching)

Take your dog for a walk. Go somewhere, perhaps by car. Begin ad-libbing freely. Spontaneously describe *everything* you see aloud. Talk about the scene—what does it look like, feel like, smell like? What do you notice most? What are you thinking when you see these things? Keep talking. Don't stop. Roll tape if that helps you. Or, make notes then edit. Eliminate the unnecessary verbiage; keep the powerful stuff.

Example:

Place and time: Sunday at the county fair.
Roll tape and talk about what you observe:

Note: *You can just talk and not use tape if that works for you.*

> "It's blazing hot—no shade anywhere. Now I'm going to have to buy one of those ridiculous hats with a pinwheel on the top. I'm starving, I ate before I left the house... watching all this food must be making me hungry, which wouldn't be so bad if the food was decent, but everything here is cooked in enough oil to run my car for a month...look at this... fried cheese...cheese is fat, frying is fat, this is fat fried in fat. I'm going to eat some anyway. Why not? Compared to all these other weird looking people, I'm Twiggy. I never saw so many huge people in my life... Maybe there was a power failure and Jerry Springer wasn't on, so they all came to the county fair to eat fried cheese. This line is fifty people long—fifty smelly, sweaty people waiting for fried cheese. Someone's kid just stuck his whole cotton candy to the back of my shirt.
>
> I'm going to the craft tent to look for my wife. She loves the craft tent, always buys something. Last year it was a plant hanger made out of fishing lures. Where is she? This is a bad sign. I don't see her. Damn, she's buying something. Whatever it is I'm going to have to say I like it. Ugh, it looks like a collage made of little pink and purple seashells. It *is* a collage made of seashells. Heaven help me, it is a picture of Elvis made of pink and purple seashells. It's fat Elvis, from Viva Las Vegas, and the jumpsuit is made out of white shells; the pink and purple ones are his cape and microphone. If she hangs it in the house, I'm sleeping in the garage."

Describe *every* little thing, no matter how inconsequential you may feel it is. Keep rolling tape. It's OK to ramble like a crazy person. This stream of consciousness exercise is just for you.

When you are done, go back to the tape, and pick out the items you thought were original, visual, and powerful. Those are the types of descriptions you'll want to use in your storytelling. Take notes if you wish. Jot down key images that will help you mentally file material that you can use on the air. You may find you only use one or two lines on your show.

Here is what ended up on a later show about "pack rats" i.e., people who collect a lot of stuff for odd reasons:

> I read an article that said people are investing in art again. It went on about how art appreciates and how you should start collecting young. I've decided we should not be collecting art in our household. My wife buys collages of Elvis. Not even thin Elvis, fat Elvis made from pink and purple seashells. Have you ever imagined spending forty dollars for a shell collage of Elvis by an up-and-coming artist? You don't imagine it. You just go to the county fair and somehow it happens. Our art collection is not going to Sothebys. It is going into a garage sale for ten cents when I die. This is not what I call a good investment.

Show Prep/Observation Worksheet

DATE: ____

TIME/PLACE: ______________________________________

OBSERVATIONS (use extra paper or roll tape): ________________

____

____

____

____

____

____

Roll tape and talk about what you observe. (You can just talk and not use tape if that works better for you.)

What you actually use from the observation tape:

Play tape/review notes.
Select three or four pieces, thoughts, or lines you think are original, visual, and powerful descriptions.

1)____

____

Show Prep/Observation Worksheet *(continued)*

2)____

____

3)____

____

4)____

____

Make notes of key images that you can use on the air.

1)____

____

2)____

____

3)____

____

Extra: Review your shows over the next few days—did any of the images, descriptions, or topic ideas turn up on the air? Which ones?

____

____

Worksheet

Show Prep/Observation Worksheet

worksheet

Exercise II

Developing Your Talent for Descriptive Detail:

GOAL: To create powerful word pictures.

This exercise improves your ability to spontaneously describe a scene or situation with specific key colorful details so that the audience "sees" what you see. Here is the method:

STEP 1: Take a look around the room. Find an object that catches your eye. It can be anything. Now describe that object with as few words as possible in three different ways.

____

____

____

STEP 2: Cut down those detailed descriptions to just the *best, most powerful image/feeling words.* Strip them to the core. Remove every unnecessary word.

____

____

STEP 3: Write or say the pared-down description. Each word used should be brightly colored as opposed to pale.

____

____

Show Prep/Observations

New Places:

Go to a new place. A store, restaurant, park, car dealership, bar, school, truck stop, event, volunteer project—any place you have not been before. **HINT:** *Try this somewhere that a person in your target audience might go.*

1) Write down one interesting or unusual thing you noticed. ________

____

____

2) Write down one piece of conversation you overheard. ________

____

____

3) Write down a description (visual) of the place itself. ________

____

____

4) Create a talkable topic or engaging question from your experience.

____

____

worksheet

Show Prep/Producer-Guests

Worksheet

Guest:

1) Who is he/she? ______________________

____

2) Why is she/he here? ______________________

____

3) What has he/she done? ______________________

____

____

4) Where does he/she live or come from? ______________________

____

____

____

5) Present materials (book, articles) about guest to host. __________
(Attach to prep worksheet)

____

____

Allow sufficient time for the host to look them over.
Note: *Some hosts need five minutes, others five days.*

Show Prep/Producer-Guests

worksheet

Check With the Host and Ask:

1) Are you intercsted? Why? What peaked your interest? (Note:This is useful when trying to get a sense of what the host might like for future shows.)

____

____

____

2) What would you like from this guest? ________________

____

____

3) Do you want him/her in the studio, by phone, or pre-taped? _____

____

____

4) How long would you like the piece to be? ______________

5) What is plan "B?" _______________________________

____

____

Before you leave the meeting/discussion, answer the host's questions and address all of the host's concerns.

Show Prep/Producer Worksheet

Worksheet

Checklist:

1) Does the host have a plan for the show? Yes_____ No _____

2) Do you know what it is? ______________________________

____

3) Have you agreed on guests, if any? ______________________

____

4) Are the guests confirmed, and did you get phone numbers where the guest(s) can be reached in the event that something changes (mobile phone, car phone, etc.)? ______________________

____

5) Do you both (all) have the schedule for guests, special events, remotes, etc.? ______________________________

____

6) Have you supplied any material for the show? ____________
(Attach to prep worksheet)

____

7) Have you discussed it with the host?____________________

____

Show Prep/Producer Worksheet *(continued)*

8) Do you both have copies of any printed material you will use?

____

9) What is your plan "B?" ___________________________

____

10) Where is the aircheck tape? Is there enough tape for the entire show? ___________________________

11) Would sound effects be helpful? Are your sound effects, music beds, and any other production elements ready to go? __________

____

12) If there have been any programming changes, does the host know about them?___________________________

____

13) Has the program director given you any special instructions? What are they? ___________________________

____

14) Have you resolved any previous problems or concerns? How?

____

worksheet

Prep—The Voice

"A man's reach should exceed his grasp."
—Robert Browning

"When you start to take this job seriously you're in trouble."
—Jimmy Buffet

"Now, What Are We Going to Do About Your Voice?"

One of the worst things I ever heard at an aircheck session was a PD asking the talent this exact question. Of course, the talent was devastated.

Fortunately, it is not your voice, but the content of what you say, that matters most. Audiences will listen to people who do not have great voices, but have something to say. They will spend very little time listening to a beautiful voice saying nothing.

Still, if you have ever gotten negative feedback about the sound of your voice, you know it can be embarrassing and frustrating. After all, what are you supposed to do about the voice you were born with? Although this workbook is *not* about the voice, there are ways to improve your voice if you want to.

Some people are lucky, like "the screecher." The screecher was a bright, talented, articulate woman whose voice made her sound as if she were on the edge of hysteria. It was painful to listen to her, although the people who tried were rewarded by an interesting viewpoint and a good sense of humor. There was a general consensus that the show would be cancelled unless the host got vocal coaching.

Finally, the desperate producer met with the PD to ask for help. "Turn up her headphones to maximum, and stick her microphone down her throat," was his advice.

The next day, four station employees literally ran into the office from their cars. "What happened to Liza? She sounds like a new person!" The improvement was instant.

Lesson: Sometimes a simple tip is all you need to sound better and fix your "voice problem."

If you are already on the radio, you probably sound OK and are likely a good verbal communicator. Much of caring for your voice is just common sense. The best advice I have been given through the years includes the following:

- **Drink a lot of water.**
- **Stand up in front of the mic (for more power and energy) instead of sitting.**
- **Relax.**
- **Speak from the diaphragm.**
- **If you *really* have a cold, stay home. You can ruin your voice by working sick. You can also take down an entire radio station by passing your illness around.**

Berkley Productions CEO and Broadcaster Susan Berkley coaches all kinds of people both on air and off. Here are some pointers from her book *Speak to Influence*, on how to unlock the hidden power in your voice. First, Susan warns what *not* to do:

Susan Berkley

Avoid:

1) **Yelling**
Some people's voices are naturally loud and booming. Until you know how to do it properly, avoid yelling whenever possible.

2) **Not being physically fit**
When your overall physical vitality is down, your voice is one of the first places it shows.

3) **Calling in to the radio station by phone**
When reporting in by phone do not speak with the phone tucked between your ear and chin. To prevent yourself from sounding like a kidnapper calling to demand a ransom, use a headset.

4) **Not warming up**
Good speech takes muscle. There are many vocal warm ups. The simplest is to hum at a comfortable pitch out loud for a few minutes before you start your day.

5) **Speaking beneath your natural pitch**
Some people habitually speak at the very bottom of their pitch range, mistakenly believing it makes them sound more authoritative and forceful. Unfortunately this puts great strain on the voice.

6) **Excessive throat clearing**
It can damage the vocal chords. Some of the reasons for excessive throat clearing are nervous habit, and allergies. If it's a nervous habit, you can break it (listen for it on your aircheck tape). Instead of clearing your throat, take a sip of water. Replace a bad habit with a good one.

Here, Susan offers practical suggestions for ten common complaints:

1) *I hate my voice. I can't believe people pay me to speak. I'm just waiting for the day they come and tell me it has all been a horrible, terrible mistake.*

Solution:

Anyone who has had any success in the entertainment field has had this thought at one time or another. The voice we hear inside our heads is not the same voice others hear when we speak. The voice you hear on tape is the way you sound to others. This can be a shock and takes some getting used to. If it's any comfort, most people hate the way they sound. Try to put these feelings aside and learn to critique your voice as if you were giving gentle feedback to your best friend. Work on your weaknesses but also appreciate your strengths. In time you'll learn to take all of this much less personally.

2) *Get that "pukin' DJ" sound out of your voice.*

Solution:

You need to sound more conversational.
Try working without headphones whenever possible. If you need them while on the air, keep the headphones on one ear only or turn the volume way down. As you listen to your aircheck, ask yourself, "Do I speak this way in normal conversation?"

The best radio creates the illusion of a one-on-one conversation between friends—not the "Voice of God" speaking to the little people from Mount Olympus.

Find a photograph of a loved one and keep it by the mic so that you can visualize speaking to that person when you're on the air. Better yet, if there's a human being in the room while the mic is on, look him/her in the eyes as you speak.

3) *Your voice sounds weak. You need more power.*

Solution:

Psyche yourself up before you go on the air. Pro athletes do it all the time. Check your posture. Use lots of body language—gesture freely with your hands. Wear comfortable clothing that doesn't restrict your breathing. Start a fitness program. To get vocal energy, you need physical energy. Eat lean before you go on the air.

4) *You sound too breathy.*

Solution:

There are two common problems with breathiness. The first is when the speaker, usually a woman, speaks in an exaggeratedly breathy manner. She often believes a breathy voice makes her sound more vulnerable and feminine.

The second problem is "misplaced breathing." The speaker exhales too much air in the middle of a thought and gives the impression that he's exhausted and gasping for breath.

Both problems can be cured by training yourself to breathe correctly and monitoring your progress with daily airchecks.

5) *You mumble. You need to improve your enunciation.*

Solution:

Vowels add color to the speech. Consonants add clarity. If people are telling you that you mumble, you are probably dropping your consonants—most commonly final 'd's, 't's, and 'g's. You're also probably speaking too fast. Short daily practice sessions with a tape recorder are needed. Read from a newspaper or book. Go slowly, making sure you enunciate clearly.

6) *Your regional accent is too strong.*

Solution:

Get a dictionary and study the diacritical markings. These will give you the correct pronunciations of the standard American vowel sounds. Practice them as best you can. Overall, this is a very difficult problem to cure without regular one-on-one sessions with an accent-reduction specialist.

7) *You don't sound warm and friendly enough.*

Solution:

This one is easy—smile. A smile on your face will put a smile in your voice. Keep a mirror near the mic to make sure there's a smile on your face whenever the mic is on.

8) *Your voice is too high.*

Solution:

Not everyone was meant to sound like James Earl Jones or Lauren Bacall. Some of us are tenors and some of us are baritones. All voices are beautiful when properly played. One of the most common causes of a high, thin voice is nervous tension. Deep abdominal breathing will help you stay relaxed so that your voice can sound its best.

9) *By the end of your show, your voice sounds tired and hoarse.*

Solution:

When you are run down, your voice is the first thing to go. If you smoke, stop immediately. If you do not smoke, avoid smoky environments like bars and clubs. Make an appointment with a throat doctor to rule out any medical problems. A healthy voice should stay strong throughout an entire airshift.

You could be suffering from allergies which could be irritating your throat. Avoid dairy products. Switch to unscented cosmetics.

Drink at least eight glasses of water a day, especially while you are on the air. Avoid ice-cold beverages — they constrict the throat muscles. Drink warm water or herb tea while on the air.

10) *Your voice sounds boring and monotonous.*

Solution:

Put the fun back in your voice. Practice reading children's stories or trashy romance novels aloud in an exaggerated manner. Work with a mirror by the mic. Do not worry if you look silly or stupid. The sillier you look, the better you will sound. If there is emotion on your face and in your eyes, we will hear it in your voice. This is radio—no one can see you anyway.

Remember, although not everyone can have a great voice, *all* voices can we worked with and improved upon.

Show Prep Notes:

Show Prep Notes:

The Powerful Radio Workbook:

Performance

The Powerful Radio Workbook:

Performance

"If you bring forth what is within you, what you bring forth will save you. If you do not bring forth what is within you what you do not bring forth will destroy you."
—Jesus

When you listen to the radio, you notice people who sound spontaneous. Like pro-athletes or prima ballerinas, they make their work look natural and easy. It seems these people never make a mistake on the air, or, if they do, the show takes an unexpected twist, and it gets even better.

Then there are broadcasters who seem pained and uncomfortable when things go astray. It can make you very nervous to listen to people reacting to a situation that way.

The difference between accomplished professionals and talented neophytes is that the seasoned air talent always give you the feeling they are in control, no matter what happens.

This skill can be learned. The people you admire on the air have mastered some basic techniques that carry them through the most difficult situations. Their experiences—successes, as well as failures, are what make them so adept now. You cannot avoid some of the unpredictable aspects of this business, but you can learn reliable techniques to improve your show. You escape certain traps by practicing a few elementary performance points, and there are things you can do to "self-correct" should the show begin to take a turn for the worse.

"To escape criticism - do nothing, say nothing, be nothing."
—William Teacher

Performance Points:

1) Pick Topics About Which You Really Care.

A great talent or personality can make selecting a sofa interesting. Boring people, on the other hand, could ruin the discovery of human life on Pluto. Interested is interesting.

2) A Strong Show Opening or Monologue Includes the Following:

- **Focus** the topic.
- **Engage** the audience by forming a question.
- **State** your opinion or position on a talkable topic.
- **Explain** your view through example, experience, or storytelling.

Do not read entire prepared speeches. If you must, do not *sound* like you are reading.

3) Never Be Boring!

Get rid of dull guests *immediately.* Remember, if you are bored, it is boring. If a guest starts out great, or was selected as an expert, but in fact turns out to be stiff, too nervous to think clearly, or is in any other way noncommunicative or inept as a storyteller, get rid of that guest.

How often have you checked your watch when a guest is talking or taken a mini-vacation in your head? If this is happening, try a few direct questions calculated to raise the energy level in the room. If that does not help, dismiss the guest.

If this is a problem for you, have a prearranged signal with your producer just as couples do at parties. Pagers help. News people can be sent in waving wire copy. Anything that allows you to shove a dullard out the door is fair. Make a transition, and immediately try doing something else.

Remember, you are probably more interesting than a boring guest. Be flexible and protect your air product. If the guest is great, keep him or her longer.

Why is this so difficult?

It is surprisingly hard to speed the departure of a guest because we are trained from childhood to consider the feelings of others. As human beings, we do not wish to be rude. But it is ultimately better to be abrupt with one guest or caller than to be impolite to an entire listening audience, boring them because we feel uncomfortable cutting off the discussion. The audience is under no obligation to be polite to you, the host. They will feel free to leave if things get dull.

But what if the expert is in the room staring at you, expecting to go on the air for the full show?

With live radio, it is especially difficult to ask the tough, meaty questions or to cut off a boring guest if that person is in the room. Do it anyway. You should not have promised a guest more than a few minutes of airtime. Your producer can explain the show's "policy" on the matter.

It is easier for some hosts to exercise the "cutoff" switch if the guest is on the telephone rather than live in the studio. Try sacrificing a little sound quality by using a phone connection if this makes it easier for you to end an interview. One famous American host has created an environment designed to simulate the listener's experience. She places the guest in another studio, without eye contact, so that the conversation relies solely on listening and verbal communication. You may find there are some advantages to conducting an interview this way.

4) Do Not Take Calls Just Because They Are There.

PD Alan Eisenson has rules for guests and callers. He says, "Guests and calls are simply tools for the host to use to make a better show. I would rather hear a strong air personality than boring callers or guests.

It is up to the host to determine when a guest or call gets boring. Some guests could be great for three hours and others are only good for five minutes. Some callers could go on for five minutes, but are only worthy of five seconds. A good host and producer should be able to tell the difference and pace the show accordingly. Only use callers to enhance the show."

5) What If the Interview or Topic Goes Wrong?

Sometimes you ask a wrong question, or don't frame your talkable topic/ engaging question well. If you are not getting the desired response, perhaps it is time to change the story or example a little, or recompose the question to engage the audience differently.

Do not be afraid to reset your topic going into or coming back from a break. But do not repeat your topic exactly. Add something new.

6) You Can Change Your Mind.

What you think is true may change. As Alan Eisenson points out, people do change.

> As an issue evolves over days or weeks, do not be afraid to change your opinion as more facts become available or if a caller or guest persuades you with a strong argument to change your mind. Do not stick to your guns if you know deep down you are wrong. Remember, always tell the truth. And don't be afraid to admit you don't know something. You're not expected to have all the facts about every issue all the time.

7) Risking on the Air.

Sometimes you head into a danger zone with a comment, view, question, or decision you make about what goes on the air. Understand that not everything you say will be popular, even if you feel it is true.

A lot of what you can get away with depends on your relationship with management. Even more depends on your level of success. Proven personalities can get away with much more than a beginning, unproven talent or a new arrival.

If you know you are heading into a "gray" area, sometimes it is better to ask permission from your boss. A powerful show is not one where a host lives in fear of getting the axe.

Note to Managers: If a talent calls you and lets you know he or she is about to move into a potentially dangerous topic, make a decision. If you need to take a moment to consult a lawyer, or another manager, do it quickly.

Is it better to beg for forgiveness than ask for permission? That depends. Trust your instinct or gut feelings, but try not to hold yourself back from potentially powerful moments. Do not be so afraid of failure or getting into trouble that you lose your spontaneity and sense of discovery, risk, or adventure on the air. Live radio is a live experience. Most times you won't go wrong when you go with what you think is right at the moment.

Remember this about CBS's Mel Karmazin: he always backs top radio performer Howard Stern. No matter what Howard says, if he gets into trouble, Mel pays the FCC fines. Mel believes in Howard and likes the profits the Stern show generates. He understands that the talent cannot be restricted. If you want the great moments, you've got to assume some risk.

The best managers behave honorably. As a manager, if you tell your talent it is OK to do a certain type of show, you are honor bound to live by that commitment until you mutually agree to change it. Do not fire talent for your mistake. If you say, "Go ahead and speak your mind, create discussion, we do not mind controversy," then be prepared for the consequences. Your phone will ring constantly with angry listeners. Your mailbox will be filled with hate letters. Fifteen people may march in front of the station, threatening to boycott your biggest advertiser, and your spouse may be embarrassed to tell friends where you work. If you are not ready to live with that on a day-to-day basis, *do not hire people who do those types of shows.*

Talent will occasionally do things you would rather they had not done. However, not all talent live on the cutting edge. Most operate somewhere between the safe and the daring. But the more artistic and creative the talent, the more risks that artist is likely to take. The payoff can be enormous, but it may cost you your serenity and security.

As you will read in the airchecking section, there are ways to guide talent to say what they want to say while generating less hostility or controversy.

It is best to establish a line of communication where managers know what is happening and can choose what fights to support. Managers do not like unpleasant surprises.

8) Use Your "Off" Switch.

From the wisdom of Jaye Albright, "Master the use of the most difficult piece of equipment in the control room: the 'off' switch on the microphone. Practice moderation. Learn to recognize when a bit is over, and stop talking at that point."

9) The Day You Wished You'd Stayed in Bed.

Not every show will be your best show. Even your favorite air personality has the occasional bad day. Sometimes you just can't hit the ball, no matter what you do. Your rhythm may be off, or you may not be feeling well.

When you have a show that did not work, it is important to do a quick analysis: Is there an easily identifiable reason you fared poorly? Not enough sleep? Hungry? Inadequate show prep? A fight with your former spouse just before you went on the air, etc. If it is fixable, fix it. Do it differently next time.

Perhaps you simply did a poor job of it. There are two things you can do: you can choose to pick it apart over and over and beat yourself with the aircheck, making yourself feel terrible, thereby ensuring you will do a worse job tomorrow, or you can let it go.

Regular listeners who like you will forgive one bad show. Tomorrow someone will be listening who has never heard you before. That person will not know about today's bad show. Forgive yourself and move forward.

10) Treat the Staff You Work With Respectfully.

Whether you know it or not, they have a lot of impact on your performance. The station staff and help you or sabotage you in a million ways. A miserable team will cost you more than you think.

Formatics

"Art lives from constraints and dies from freedom."
—Leonardo da Vinci

Listeners like formatics. They provide structure, like the walls of a house. People want to know to whom and what they are listening, and they like to know what time it is.

Jaye Albright says;

> For most of us in most situations, I consider formatics to be absolutely essential. They are like "the blocking and tackling" exercises of our sport. And, as in the NFL—where they begin spring drills with the statement, "This is a football," before you dispense with them, you must execute them naturally, flawlessly.
>
> Formatics are all about memorability, habit and familiarity. It is these things that make ratings, unless your content is constantly superior and compelling.

For a programmer, making sure the formatics are properly done is the easiest part of an aircheck session. The tape tells all. If anything is missing after a performance, follow it up with an aircheck session. Call attention to it and make it a goal for the next session.

Sometimes new talent do not understand the importance of formatics to ratings diaries. Explain the necessity of getting this part right by showing the talent actual sample diary pages. Here is one element of getting ratings that is up to each host. Because we live and die by Arbitron's research diary methods, it makes sense to do everything we know to win the roulette game of ratings. Repetition stimulates recall. It is that simple.

Even if your program director or manager does not hound you about formatics, it is in your best interest to do them. Take the initiative. Be responsible for eliminating what Arbitron terms "Phantom Cume"—i.e., those people who listen but can't exactly remember the dial position, call letters or name of your station.

"Why must I hammer these call letters over and over again? Don't people already know what they are listening to?"

I once consulted a station with famous historic call letters. Everyone associated with it was proud to work for this radio legend. They assumed people were familiar with their station. Many were, but most of their actual listeners seldom heard the call letters or station name, and had trouble remembering where they were tuned.

We increased that station's ratings 70% in one ratings period, by saying the call letters, and the name of the station, every time we took a call, gave the time, started the news, opened the microphone. I would love to say we added 70% to our listening audience, but the truth of the matter is, we simply made it easier for people writing in their Arbitron diaries to remember where they were tuned. You can never say the call letters too many times.

Every fifteen minutes you are judged by what the diary keepers write down. That means *every fifteen minutes* hammer home:

- **YOUR NAME**
- **NAME OF THE SHOW**
- **NAME OF THE STATION ("THE TALK STATION")**
- **CALL LETTERS AND DIAL POSITION**

Repetition is the way we learn and memorize. Think of television's *Sesame Street*. Repeat and repeat and repeat until the audience gets it.

Talk Radio Formatics

Each format in radio has slightly different formatics. For talk radio, the structure is more or less like the one Alan Eisenson uses:

1) **Open the hour with your name, the time, and the call letters.** This is basic formatics which is a separate issue from content execution.

2) **Do some short opening comments,** if you have any that day which may or may not be your main topic.

3) **Launch into your monologue,** i.e., engage the audience with your opinion/position and storytelling.

4) **Ask the question.** This is your tightly focused topic.

5) **Give out the phone numbers.**

6) **Take a break,** using proper formatics.

7) **Open the flood gates** (the phones) **after your first break.**

8) **Reset the topic by asking the question going in and out of each subsequent break** (again, using proper formatics).

If you have successfully hooked the audience with your monologue, talkable topic or engaging question, you should have sufficient calls for the entire hour.

Overcoming Resistance

Programmers around the world share a common frustration and ask the same question of talent: "Why don't you simply do the formatics as you are told? How hard can this be? We have talked about this over and over again!"

Talent says: "You care more about call letters and time checks than you do about content! A monkey or a robot could do formatics. I am an individual. I got involved in what was happening at the moment."

Some managers take it too far and become obsessive about the number of call letter and dial position mentions. Although it is my belief that you can never say the name enough times, WPLJ/New York PD Scott Shannon has an important point. He reminds programmers: "Great stations are not built on hot clocks, and contests, they are built on heart."

Why rebel with formatics or forget to do them? The reason is that talent does not believe it is important. Because they already know where they work, it is boring to them to repeat the station's dial position and call letters.

In order to get the talent to comply, good managers have to explain why call letters are so vital. Remember that although the formatics do not make great radio, they are an important element which can aid you in increasing your ratings. If the talent does not understand the absolute importance of formatics, they will *not* be a priority. If your staff is in formatic rebellion, then you have not properly communicated that, without formatics, someone else will get the credit for their great show.

Hosts do not want to be good little soldiers and just follow orders. They hate being told what to do without a reason. But the reasons for formatics are all to their advantage. People tend to act in their own best interests. As a last resort, if a talent continually forgets to do formatics, try helping out with produced elements.

It is to everyone's benefit if talent understands how listeners listen. Make it clear that the audience has a short attention span and often uses radio as background.

Resetting and Teasing

Radio Computing Service manager Tom Zarecki spent years as a programming consultant. He says:

> Since new people keep tuning in, the host needs to frequently recap guest's names, what group they represent, and the topic. Keep teasing upcoming show segments or features. Waiting five minutes in a drive-time interview to recap what's going on, or only teasing once or twice an hour, is simply not often enough.
>
> If you expect your listeners to remember your name and call letters for ratings purposes, then it's pretty important to hammer in those call letters. Take the time to explain.

Formatics do not have to be dry and boring; in fact, if you do them well, they become a creative and exciting part of your show.

I know a music station where all the live talk is entirely formatics. There isn't much room for creativity. One DJ has to give *sixteen* weather reports each day. That is, four times an hour, four hours a day, five days a week. He works in Los Angeles, where the weather rarely changes. This DJ's secret dream was to be a television weather reporter. He loves doing the weather and makes it the most creative part of his show: "Aren't you glad you got that haircut? It is going to be another scorcher today..." With a little effort, you can make formatics more interesting than they seem.

Formatic Tips from Tommy Kramer

Tommy suggests:

> Be sensitive to repetition. A good talent varies the way everything is done. The listener wants consistency but not predictability. Even if positioning phrases or branding should require that things be said in the same words all the time, the talent can still vary the inflection of the words. Repetition becomes boring quickly and is also an indicator of the deadly 'automatic pilot' mentality that can bring down a talent or a station fast. Do your part. Keep the talent energized by pointing out good examples when they occur, or freshening things up that may have become tired sounding.

Tommy also recommends some specific ways to use formatics to engage your audience:

> Pull the listener into the radio with you. If you say 'It's 72 degrees out there' you tell me, the listener, that I'm out there and you are not out there with me. You are somewhere else. In reality, I am in my car or at my desk and you are with me when I am listening. Why push me away? I've heard talent in Fort Worth [a suburb of Dallas, Texas] say 'over in Fort Worth...' Why? Just saying 'in Fort Worth' will say it without distancing yourself from the Fort Worth listener. Avoid saying anything that pushes the listener away.

Sell the Benefit.
Always sell a benefit of the show or station. "Soft easy favorites" is not a reason for me to listen to you on my way home from work. What is the benefit to me? But "soft easy favorites to make your drive home easier" gives me a reason to listen.

Use Real Language.
What is more effective? "For further information and details call 456-1111" or "You want to know more? Give me a call." How about "It's just about forty five minutes after the hour of twelve o'clock..." Would you ever say that if I asked you what time it was? Wouldn't you just glance at your watch and say 12:45? Talk on the air the way you talk in life.

Connect with the Listener.
Tell me—don't read to me. Let your language and manner pull the listener into the radio. Newsman Paul Harvey writes about a dozen key words on a card, and tells you the story.

The Rule of One.
Do one main thing per break.
Obviously, you need to identify the station and/or music, give the time and whatever your station's "formatics" are, but do that stuff briefly and then do the one thought you set out to do this break.

Hit the Target.
Draw up a specific profile of your listener, complete with a picture if possible. Post it in the on-air studio. Speak to that one target listener every time the mike opens. Say things that will appeal to and interest him or her. For instance if it is a soft adult contemporary station, you

might not want to dwell on the hockey scores. And keep it singular. Do not say, "If some of you listening would like to go..." Instead say, "If you want to go..." Always aim at the target.

- **Promote Ahead.**
  Promote anything of benefit coming up on your show. Be truthful. Instead of "I'll have tickets to give away in a few minutes," try "This hour, you'll have a chance to win James Taylor tickets!"

  If you tell me something is coming up in a few minutes and I only have twenty minutes until I get to work, I'll be mad at you if you don't get to it by the time I shut off the car radio. But if you tell me it's coming up within the next thirty minutes, and I only have twenty, I won't hold it against you. Never promote anything as, "coming up after the break." That is like saying, "I'm going away now."

- **Don't Tell the Listener What to Think.**
  It is irritating. "Here's one you'll really like" (How do you know? What if I don't?) or "you'll have a great time" (what if I have a lousy time?). Tell me that you like it and why (or why some people like it). Let me decide for myself.

- **Sell the Dream First, Then Give the Information.**
  In advertising, they say, "sell the sizzle not the steak." Seek an emotional link with the listener. Help me see why I want to win before I have to hear all the junk about how to do it. If you do not make me want what is being offered, there is no reason for me to care about all that technical information.

Have a Road Map.
Know how you are starting. Have a destination in mind. Know how you are ending. Move on to the next element.

Often a talent takes way too long to get to the point. We have all heard breaks like: "WZXT 99 with Elton John and Rocket Man from 1973. You know, he's done a lot of great work over the years and this one is definitely one of the all time favorites. Now let's go to the phones—Jennifer's on line three. Let's find out what her most embarrassing moment was. Jennifer, how are you this morning?" Tighten it up, cut to the chase! "WZXT 99 with Elton John and Jennifer is on the phone. Jennifer, what embarrassed you the most?"

How to Edit Phone Calls.
Keep the unnecessary parts of the calls off the air. "OK, Jane, thanks for calling in today, or thanks for having me on, taking my call," and other superfluous stuff does not need to be on the air. It is boring, slows momentum, and no one cares. Instead identify the station and keep to the point, "Jane you are on Sunny 98.5. What weird gift did you get on your birthday?"

Reset the Stage.
Adopt an egg-timer attitude, and every couple of minutes briefly reset the stage for anyone who may just be joining the show. [One talent coach I know actually leaves a fifteen-minute hourglass on the studio console.] If the listener cannot quickly get what is going on, he or she might choose another station. If I tune in and hear "Florida coach Steve Spurrier on Sports Radio 540, The Team," this morning, I won't feel confused. Let the new listener know which voice belongs to which person and what that person's role is! "Celluloid Mike, our film critic is here. Mike what should I take the kids to see this weekend?"

DENNIS THE MENACE

"I LIKE THE WAY YOU DON'T EVER TAKE A BREAK FOR COMMERCIALS."

Break the Habit of "Taking a Break"

Please do not use the word "break." It comes from TV, where they regularly *do* stop the action and do other things. Because everything on your radio station is a part of your total format, you are almost never "breaking away."

Do not "break now for the news." Each time you tell the audience there is a break, they think that they, too, can "break away." The whole show is yours. That includes spots, news, and anything else inside your show. Stations are rated not only on how many listeners show up, but also on how many listeners stick around. Try something along the lines of "Let's find out what else is going on. It's 6:00 and you are listening to WXXX. News is next." Do not throw away a single minute of your airtime, even if your station requests that you give a standard introduction to other elements. The mark of a professional is the ability to make every word his or her own.

Do Not Panic If You Need a Moment

Have you ever heard someone on the radio chattering aimlessly, verbally casting about for clarity of thought or direction? That talent has likely been taught "Keep the meter moving. Whatever else happens, keep talking."

However, that fear of "dead air" can provoke meaningless, manic episodes that will actually lose your audience. Do not be afraid of a moment of silence. The listeners will understand, and it beats the alternative. Do not panic. Take a pause if you need a few seconds to collect your thoughts.

Taking a moment of silence can also become a tool. Veteran New York radio host Bob Grant learned this trick and often pauses for a few seconds after he states a powerful message to get the listener's attention. Grant, among others, has learned that nothing gets the attention of the listeners more quickly than a second or two of "dead air."

Content + Formatics = Ratings

In addition to your content and style, here are some talk-radio basic formatics that can make a difference (and get you ratings).

Before each break:

- Remember to tease what is coming up or reset your talkable topic or engaging question.
- Involve your audience. Use a cliff-hanger to keep them coming back for more, staying through a break, or just listening longer.

Here is an example of a reset that reminds the audience of the topic under discussion:

> "In case you've just joined us, I am James Johnson and you are listening to WXYZ AM 690. Our guest is supermodel Christie Christensen, talking about her new book, *"Sleep your way to the top*." What do you think? Is it OK to use sex to get your next job? Here's our number, 666-8255..."

A reset should include:

- **YOUR NAME**
- **STATION**
- **TOPIC**
- **DIAL POSITION**
- **ASK FOCUSED QUESTION OR TEASE**
  Preferably one that everyone listening to *will* have a burning desire to answer.
- **PHONE NUMBER**
- **GO TO COMMERCIALS OR SERVICE ELEMENTS**

Performance Notes:

Performance Notes:

Performance Notes:

The Powerful Radio Workbook:

Post Production Planning

The Powerful Radio Workbook:

The Aircheck Session

"No one can make you feel inferior without your consent."
—Eleanor Roosevelt

Talent Are Hungry for Feedback

Surprisingly, hosts often hire me at their own expense to conduct aircheck sessions with them, craving direction that their program directors cannot or do not have time to give.

Airchecking is more than just a "tape critique." One-on-one coaching, or airchecking, is a specific, focused way of working. It is not the only tool that can be used to develop, improve, and advance talent, but it is the best way. Airchecking is the process of listening to tape of a show and, using specific criteria, determining what worked and what did not work. With a guide, airchecker, coach, or PD as your witness, one then decides what can be improved.

Even if you listen to tape of your shows religiously, you are likely to miss many nuances of the total performance. One air talent I work with says, "When I listen alone, I focus on how *I* did. I get critical of just me, not how the whole show went. When I listen with other people in the room, I focus on *everything* that is happening on the air: the guest being interviewed, sound effects, callers, spot breaks, etc. I hear it all."

It can't be helped. Think of your school or family group photos. When you see one, the first thing you do is look at yourself. It is the same in radio. The natural thing is to pay attention to how you made a certain point or handled a particular caller. You are less likely to be aware of the subtleties of that caller's comments or the newsperson's clever contribution. There is something about listening to your show with a *witness* in the room that forces you to hear your work differently. The goal of airchecking is to aircheck in such a way that each talent sets achievable goals to fulfill his or her creative potential.

The Mirror

Talent, if you do not know what you sound like on the air, you are already in the danger zone. You are working with a handicap.

Watch a child play by making faces in a mirror. What do I look like if I'm mad? What do I look like with my tongue out? Can I see myself from the back?

Airchecking is like a mirror. How do I sound when I am sad or angry? How do I behave with a difficult guest? What happens when I try to sound smarter than my partner? Am I smarter than my partner? What happens when I pretend to know something about a topic I know nothing about? What happens when I'm bored on the air? How do I sound if I didn't get enough sleep? What kind of a show will I have if I have not been out of my house in a month except to go to work?

Your audience knows, but without your aircheck tape as a mirror, you do not. Sitting alone with a tape of your show is like a single mirror. Working with a talented aircheck coach can give you multiple reflections of your work. There are other angles you cannot see with only one frame of reference. Viewing those other angles is the power of a good aircheck session.

What Exactly Is an Aircheck?

That depends. One New York DJ defines an aircheck session as "a way for the program director to yell at us periodically." Says another: "Isn't it like a report card?" From a manager, "Oh yes, we do that once a year with talent. We analyze a tape of a show. The meeting takes an entire day. You can read the report in their file." And one industry professional simply asked: "Isn't it some kind of post-mortem after a dead show?"

These comments all have a grain or two of truth, but try thinking of your show as a garden and airchecking the show as a weeding process. In order to maintain its health, growth, and beauty, you should regularly walk through your garden taking note of which plants are thriving and which need attention. Some parts of the garden flourish, some struggle to survive. Always you appreciate its beauty. If there is a special new plant in your garden, you want to learn its potential and create the right environment for it to grow. You make sure it has the right sun, soil, etc. Your aircheck is like that walk to see how well your garden is coming along.

When done correctly, airchecking can be a solution to the dilemma facing managers and programmers around the world who complain: "I can't find any good talent. I've listened to dozens of tapes and they are all bad or mediocre. Or, "This is a good station in a reasonably sized market, and the job pays a decent salary. Why can't we find the right people?"

Exactly where are all those talented and creative people hiding? Where is the next generation of talent? You may get lucky and find a genius on the doorstep of your radio station, but one important task of radio programmers and managers is to find and develop new personalities. Airchecking is an excellent solution to the problem.

Basic Aircheck Rules

"One must be permitted to be clumsy and fail..."
—May Sarton

1) **Always have a tape of the show you are discussing on hand.** You may wish to transcribe it word for word to emphasize specifics. Keep in mind that a transcript can destroy context, i.e., sarcasm, irony, humor all get left behind with the loss of vocal inflection. This often happens when a manager receives a nasty call or complaint letter with specific quotes included. Inevitably the context is missing. A discussion can degenerate quickly if the actual facts of the case are in dispute. Having the tape allows you not only to look at the content, but also the context of an event on the show.

2) **Focus on one thing at a time.** Sometimes an aircheck session turns into a "dump" session, in which talent unburdens him or herself of a lot of thoughts having nothing to do with the show. A double standard applies here. It's acceptable, to a point, for the host to digress. After all, a PD is uniquely able to understand pressures talent may be under, and even, in some cases, to do something to alleviate them. As a manager, however, you are there to aircheck, not to vent. Listen to the talent. Should you hear the makings of a great show taking place in your office, encourage the talent to put that on the air.

   Don't let these diversions distract you from the aircheck session; just move the subject back to the tape and the show at the most appropriate moment.

3) **Tell the truth.**
Trained communicators sense when you are fibbing.

4) **Reinforce the positive by starting with the good stuff.**
Remember to acknowledge goals achieved.

5) **Be fair.**
Criticism goes in very deep. No matter how angry you are, avoid verbalizing your negative reactions to a piece until you can express yourself calmly and rationally.

6) **Let the talent discover along with you what needs to be improved.**

7) **Outline strengths. Ask a lot of questions.**
What worked? Why did you want to do this on the radio? What were you trying to say here? Did this connect? Did this make you laugh?

8) **Have faith.**
Believe in your talent's ability to improve.

9) **Always end an aircheck session with one or two mutually agreed upon "Achievable Goals."**
Pick at least one thing that can easily be accomplished by the next scheduled session. Try to let the talent initiate goal-setting if possible.

10) **Is there anything on the tape that you could use as a promo?**

The Method: How To Aircheck

"Managing creative people is an oxymoron. You don't manage them at all. Instead you provide an environment in which they can be simultaneously stimulated and protected, challenged and encouraged, exposed and private.
—Nicholas Negroponte

Unfortunately, there is no airchecking school for programmers. One learns by working with people, seeing what is effective and what is not. Some aspects of airchecking will vary greatly, depending upon the individuals involved. It is in the best interest of programmers and managers to learn to aircheck effectively. If the talent wins, the station wins. There are a few things one must *never* do, but the only *right* way to aircheck is the way that *works*.

In the United States, where it is becoming easier and less expensive to take a syndicated network show than to have local live talent on the air, it is critical that we develop new talent now. Most syndicated programs were once local success stories. Someone worked with each of those hosts when they were starting out.

Even the strongest syndicated shows can be beaten by hot local talent. I frequently meet novice broadcasters with much to offer. What will stations do once today's syndicated shows run dry or move to television? We need to look to the future. Airchecking and developing these talented people is one way to ensure that creative and powerful radio will continue into the next generation. Of course, after a few years of experience, some of these very people will go on to become major syndicated talent.

Without an understanding of what is required for an individual air talent to succeed, even the most gifted new hire may not reach his or her potential. In a case like that, it takes a year or two for the talent to leave or be asked to move on. What went wrong?

Let's go back to the garden analogy. You came home from the garden center with some big, fancy bulbs. The picture on the box showed a huge, exotic flower, but, unfortunately, the box was without instructions. How much water was needed? How much sun?

There may have been nothing wrong with the talent you chose, but when you have to play a guessing game with insufficient information there is a good chance of damaging the talent, or at least failing to create an environment where talent, like that fancy flower, can blossom.

If you found something you did not recognize in your garden, you would not cut it back without knowing what it was. It could be something wonderful. The same goes for air talent. Consultant Dan Vallie, puts it well when he advises programmers to "let talent go out on a limb as far as they can. Do not restrict them until you find their range of potential and limitations. It's better to reel them in after a while than to have to keep pushing them out there."

Fix It Today

A great aircheck session with a trained program director can move talent along faster than any other tool. Progress may be painstakingly slow. Talent improves step by step, day by day. Frustratingly, the process may sometimes seem to be working in reverse. There is a period of intense growth, followed by what sound like patches of mediocrity, where all coaching seems to have been in vain. What you may really be hearing is the talent searching for ways to implement suggestions and ideas you have discussed. Have faith and continue the process. If you are on the right path, positive change will come.

Dan Vallie

Several other experts have contributed their aircheck rules and philosophies to the workbook, including Dan Vallie with Vallie-Richards Consulting. He is a big believer in spending time to coach talent.

Here are a few of Dan's steps to talent development:

1) Talent is the product. You can't develop talent if you do not spend time together. The talent will improve more quickly if time is taken for coaching and direction.

2) Do not criticize talent or tell them something was poorly done unless you direct them on how to do it better. If you cannot give them a better way, at least approach the issue with a team attitude, working together to come up with a solution.

3) Do not let the aircheck session become, or be perceived as, a waste of time by talent. Make yourself part of the show, as the director. Directing involves making sure the talent play to their strengths. Help to assist and make up for their weaknesses. Give guidance in those periods where the talent is at a loss of how to grow next or how to handle an immediate topical event on the air.

4) If the expectation is not clear, the delivery will not be on target.

5) You can learn from the talent, just as the talent can learn from you. Do not direct by doing all the talking. It is frequently more important to listen. Be sincerely interested in the talents' views and understand their perspectives.

6) Be a good facilitator. Draw talent out and get them to verbalize their feelings and thoughts. Watch their body language. Show them that you care about them and the show's success.

7) If yours is a music-intensive station with most of the personalities on the morning show, meet with them every day. It does not have to be an aircheck session. The format and length of the meeting can vary. If everyone sees it as helpful, you will all make time to meet. If any of you thinks it is a waste, the meeting will frequently be cancelled or dreaded.

8) Do not try to impress the talent with how much you know, where you have worked, or that fact that you are the boss. Just be honest, encouraging, supportive, and consistent with your direction and approach.

9) Great coaches give talent credit when they perform and share the blame when something fails. These are the people who can get you to the superbowl or hall of fame, but only when you work as a team.

10) Praise often in public and private—but criticize only in private.

It Cuts Both Ways

Mistakes occur when an aircheck session is mishandled. Just as a talent can get a reputation for being difficult to work with, your reputation as a programmer can be severely damaged by a bad relationship with a host in your employ. These people do talk to one another and to managers. It is possible that the person whose aircheck session you botched years ago can keep you from getting your next job or warn away a show you are actively courting.

There are a lot of ways to mess up an aircheck session. If you have worked in the business for a while, you are probably familiar with some of them. Lorna Ozmon, president of Ozmon Media, provides an all-too-accurate picture of what can go wrong:

> Let's examine the state of the art model for critiquing air personalities. Typically air personalities are critiqued, on average, monthly. The aircheck sessions are often canceled or rescheduled due to an "emergency" usually having to do with sales. The talent and the PD meet in the PD's office with all its inherent disruptions and distractions. The talent hands the PD a tape of a show the PD has never heard, which the PD puts in the tape machine behind him or her.
>
> As the tape begins to play the PD is thinking, "I hope I can come up with something to say and not look like I have nothing of value to offer." The talent is thinking, "I hope this is over soon and it doesn't hurt my feelings." After a few breaks, the PD stops the tape and, with a quizzical look, says, "There's something about that break that bothers me." At this the talent silently wonders, "What does that mean?" and says, "Could you give me something a little more specific?"

Feeling slightly inadequate, the PD gives the talent a healthy dose of "don'ts" and sends the talent out feeling confused, unmotivated, clear on what *not* to do but clueless about what *to* do. This traditional approach to airchecks has done much to close the minds and hearts of talent at radio stations everywhere.

How Airchecking Can Damage Talent

Lorna Ozmon takes a psychological approach to airchecking and has developed her own techniques. She has found that before she can begin to make progress with a talent, it is essential to explore what has been said to him or her over the years that created both the good and bad habits he or she carries. Lorna's cardinal rule for airchecking comes from Hippocrates: "Make a habit of two things—to help or at least do not harm."

Ozmon explains:

> Before talent can move forward, you've got to get rid of the unnecessary baggage, stuff they've been told by bad PDs or people who influenced them when they were just starting out. That stuff really sticks.
>
> I usually ask them to make a list of all the "orders" they have been given through the years. Then we look at the list and ask "What no longer works?"
>
> The idea is to get rid of the "old tapes" from previous programmers. Old-time journeymen broadcasters have been hammered by dozens of PDs. It is time to get rid of what no longer works for the

Lorna Ozman

> talent. It is not enough to haul out the clichés and tell talent to "be an individual," "just be yourself," or "be more conversational."
>
> In order to be effective, you have to be very specific when you guide talent. You have to ask questions and point out to talent what you hear and what you think it means.

Ozmon particularly warns against the "Frankenstein Syndrome," which she calls "pieces of others." She advises: "It is OK to use *tactics* learned from others, but do not cobble together pieces of what works for other people and imitate it. That *doesn't* work."

Ozmon continues:

> There is much harm being done to the performances, psyches and potential of air personalities today. Management tends to forget that people who are asked to risk parts of who they are every day must be managed differently than those who work on the assembly line at a Detroit automotive plant.
>
> Many air personalities are now being managed by cops, not coaches. Cops punish people for mistakes and misjudgments. Coaches train, instruct, and inspire new behavior. Cops tells us what *not* to do. Coaches explain what *to* do and demonstrate *how* to do it. The result of the "cop mentality" in radio air personality development is a lot of time wasted in attempting talent development with disappointing on-air results.

What follows are ten complaints from air talent who have expressed to Lorna Ozmon what they feel is wrong with the traditional "aircheck" or "tape critique" process:

Ten talent complaints about traditional airchecking:

1) **No or too few aircheck sessions.**

2) **Contradictory or inconsistent input.**

3) **Lack of praise for progress.**

4) **All negative feedback.**

5) **Lack of "how to's" and creative input.**

6) **Vague input without specific examples.**

7) **Autocratic edicts without rationale to support or explain them.**

8) **Perceived personal attacks.**

9) **Criticism from a higher authority delivered as though it came from the program director.**

10) **Program directors who critique dishonestly, either because they do not believe a personality fits their station, or do not believe in his or her ability to succeed.**

Lorna Ozmon's list spells out the damage that can be done to talent. Clearly, air personalities who have experienced some of these difficulties will be less trusting of the process than those with positive airchecking experiences.

A Cautionary Tale

Here is what can happen when you ignore the preceding list:

'John' considers aircheck sessions just this side of a torture chamber. He has good reason.

> "I know my PD uses these aircheck meetings to jerk me around. He makes me feel small, and he gets off on belittling me. He keeps these stupid lists of minutiae. I dread these meetings. They wreck my whole day. I hate being airchecked. Even if I make a change, he never says anything positive about my work. I'm not convinced my PD knows why my show works when it does. I wish he would leave me alone. I get ratings, and I have been doing this for years."

If John works for you, you are either a sadist or something is terribly wrong with your airchecking technique. Because they are already in a very vulnerable situation, talent should be made to feel as much in control of their sessions as possible. Here is how:

- Let the talent choose the tape.
- If there are notes from the session, let the talent keep them.
- Give the talent access to positive feedback from anyone whose input is going to matter during the session.
- Always acknowledge progress and positive changes.

There are differing opinions as to the benefit of revealing research results to talent. Be careful. You do not want to withhold information, but you do not want to beat talent down with the ratings book so that they become discouraged. Consultant Randy Lane, head of the Randy Lane Company, advises: "Keep the emphasis on the performance, regardless of the numbers." If there is a reason you are calling a meeting, let your talent know, if possible, what it is.

Why Don't More Programmers Aircheck? Here Are a Few of the Million Reasons:

1) **No time**
It takes as much as a two hour session for each hour of tape.

2) **Emotionally draining**
You are dealing with people's personal qualities and deepest feelings.

3) **No confidence**
Most programmers have little training in this area and fear doing harm. Also, talent can get pretty defensive about their work. Lorna Ozmon counsels PDs to prepare for this using a tactic called "Objection Busting." She says, "You must mentally prepare for every possible objection to what it is you are trying to sell. In the case of an aircheck session, it is usually a change in behavior. If you have a logical response to every reason why the talent does not agree with your position, you will be more relaxed, focused, and effective while conducting your aircheck sessions."

4) **No crisis**
Some only aircheck when things go drastically (think lawsuit) wrong.

5) **Burnout**
Most PDs are overworked and overwhelmed with demands for their attention. (See reasons #1 and #2.)

6) **Don't like them**
Sometimes management has a show or host that they find personally distasteful.

Using these reasons, many PDs recite an internal monologue like this one:

"Who am I to pick apart this show? These guys are professionals and have been doing it pretty well for a long time. I don't want to say anything to them that will break their stride. I know the show isn't as good as it could be, but I'm not sure why. What if I'm just pick-pick-picking on the little stuff? What if I'm wrong? What if I antagonize them? Then they will rebel and won't do anything I want them to do. I'm better off leaving them alone."

The end result of this internal discussion is that the aircheck session never happens, and the talent is deprived of an opportunity to improve his or her craft.

For program directors, the first step in making an effort at airchecking is acknowledging your areas of discomfort. Trust and truth must be established from both sides. This book cannot help you if you do not have good faith, a kind heart, and a desire to help your talent improve. If you are willing to overcome your resistance to airchecking, the rewards can be great. If you simply want a quick and easy way to strong-arm a performer into giving you the show you want to hear, this book won't do you any good.

Do not attempt to manipulate talent with false praise or threats. It is not right, it is not fair, and most of these folks are smart enough to know what you are doing. If you can only do one thing in your first aircheck session, pick out something on the tape you really did like and be specific about why. That would be an excellent start.

Knowing When the Time Is Right

Managers can aid talent by being sensitive to the right time for an aircheck. Educators call it the "teachable moment." Aircheck regularly at a mutually agreed upon date and place. As a guideline for newer talent, plan on a weekly session. Those getting started tend to require more attention from programmers, while more seasoned professionals may only need periodic airchecking to stay on track.

For talent who are not used to airchecking, the very idea of having to go through tape for a PD can be unsettling. That is why Tommy Kramer suggests:

> Have your talent tape every show. That way, you will always have a current tape and your talent will get relaxed with the idea of having a tape rolling. Plus, if something great happens on the air, you can have it on hand for a promo or sales presentation.

Lorna Ozmon feels strongly that full-time personalities should be airchecked once a month. She says:

> Air personalities need time to process input and put it into practice for a reasonable period of time before they are ready to tackle a new concept or take the next step. Try to, as much as is operationally possible, make monthly sessions firm commitments. Although air personalities may say they dislike the aircheck process, nothing makes them feel less valued than cancelling meetings with them.

For music program directors, Randy Lane uses this rule of thumb, "Have as much contact with your morning show as you do with the music and promotion directors." I agree with Andy Beaubien when he says:

> It is more desirable to briefly connect with an air talent on a very frequent basis than to rely on extended but infrequent meetings. The important thing is to maintain a continuing relationship. Some meetings should be in-depth discussions, while others may be brief and social in nature. Artistic growth can only come from the development of one's talents. Too often, once all the negatives in a person's style have been eliminated, there is nothing left but a bland and lifeless corpse.

Create a Safe Setting

For some, that may mean in a private office across a desk. Others prefer sitting at a restaurant with a glass of wine or cup of coffee. It does not have to be formal, but it does have to be regular and consistent.

Lorna Ozmon suggests:

> Get away from your phone, the sales department, and other distractions. Focus only on the air personality and the review. Go somewhere quiet and private enough to conduct the sessions effectively. Also, look for opportunities to be among people and observe life in your market at the same time. Meet over a meal if possible. People tend to be much more open to ideas when they are being fed.

Set the Scene

RCS consultant and former PD Tom Zarecki points out, *"The goal is to get the talent to enjoy aircheck sessions."* He agrees that the setting for an aircheck is crucial. These are his thoughts on the subject:

> Meet in a private area. Airchecking is a personal thing to the person whose voice is on the tape. If you have an office, close the door and put a sign on it saying "Aircheck session in progress. Do not disturb." Alert the front desk to hold your calls.
>
> If you don't have a private area, use your car. Sit in the parking lot or go for a drive and critique the tape along the way. No interruptions, no calls, very private. In case the talent needs to raise his or her voice, other staffers will not hear yelling from behind a closed door, which fosters gossip.
>
> Never go through a host's tapes with other hosts present. The only time aircheck sessions should be in a group is with a team show, like a morning show, where two or more people interact. Otherwise, do not review airchecks at an air-talent meeting. It is fatal. Don't try it.

Tom Zarecki

What Can Kill a Session

The absolute worst thing you can do is turn a session into a personal attack. No matter what you have to say to an air talent, if he or she feels berated or treated disrespectfully you will make no progress at all.

Randy Lane agrees, saying, "Do not use a confrontational approach, it will not inspire performance." Lorna Ozmon advises, "If you are not clear of the difference between an assertive and aggressive statement, remember it is easy to add the words, 'you idiot' to an aggressive statement. Continually remind your air personalities that it is *what they do* on the air and not *who they are* that is being airchecked."

1) Avoid airchecking just prior to the show.

It always takes some time to digest new information, and, if the session was disturbing in any way, it could hurt today's show.

2) Never ever, *ever* hotline a talent during his or her show.

Resist the temptation unless your station's license is in jeopardy or lives are at stake. Receiving a "hotline call" from the boss during the show is a sure way to frighten the host and throw the remainder of the program off rhythm. This is to be avoided at all costs. Even if the manager is calling with praise (and you should), it destroys the host's concentration. The right time to aircheck or make any comments is once the show has concluded. If the show takes place outside of normal business hours, make an extra effort to aircheck at the host's convenience. Be flexible. Many top programmers are willing to come in on the weekends.

3) Don't build unnecessary resentment.

Be sensitive to your talent's schedules. For example, do not ask your overnight host to appear at a noon meeting when he or she would normally be asleep. If you aircheck the morning show, do not pounce on your team as they leave the studio. You are just getting to the station, but after five hours on the air it is their lunchtime. They are probably hungry. They might be more receptive to your comments if their stomachs are full. Try taking them out or ordering breakfast. Hosts appreciate your willingness to take their odd hours into consideration.

PERHAPS NOW WE COULD TALK ABOUT THE SHOW

Why do we need aircheck sessions, and what can be accomplished by doing them?

Sometimes managers need to be reeducated in order to learn that what they have on the air is a work-in-progress, not a finished product, and that the show will most likely develop and get a lot better in the weeks and months to come.

All too often programmers hire and fire talent without ever having invested the time and energy that might have made a good host great, or enabled a talent to see the power of his or her work as well as its shortcomings.

If you are a radio program manager, and your air talent asks you, "What did you think of the show?" and you either: didn't hear it; did hear it, but didn't like it (but can't pinpoint *exactly* why...); or do not have time to deal with it now. This is the time to schedule an aircheck meeting.

Dan Vallie warns, "Do not make generic comments like 'good show' when you did not hear it."

Airchecking is hard and takes a lot of time.
Isn't there an easier way to develop talent?

Airchecking gets easier the more experience the talent and the coach have with it. Consultant Dan Vallie reminds us *"Coaching takes talent, too."*

Airchecking is the power of one on one. It's being heard. It is someone for you, on your side. In athletics it is the coach who pushes the athlete to maximum potential. Exercise makes sore muscles, but in the end it is worth it when you win.

Not only will you be pushing the talent on your staff to excel, but they will also be pushing you. A healthy aircheck session frequently features some strong differences of opinion. Most experts believe this should be encouraged.

Jaye Albright works with personalities who have differing styles and goals. She tries to help the talent pursue these goals for their shows. In her words:

> At best, I hope to get the personalities talking about what they were trying to do. That way, I can base my feedback on how well they accomplished what they wanted to do in terms of my responses. I try to communicate one or two key reactions I had in as nonthreatening a manner as possible. It is not important to me that they always do what I suggest, but it is important that they know why I feel as I do.
>
> I ask that they hold me to the same standard. Was I prepared or on autopilot? Did I offer clichés, or did I spend time thinking about the work? I hope they will be as direct about these things with me as I try to be with them.
>
> The longer I have worked with someone and the better I know them, the more I tailor what I do to his or her communication style. Some people are so controlling that critiques only happen on their turf, and they change very little over the years on the things I fervently believe would benefit the individual.
>
> In these cases, I keep singing my song to them in hopes that eventually the air talent will realize that there is a recurring theme in my advice and perhaps some grain of my truth will imprint.

> In other, more common situations, even the slightest word can injure. In those situations, I attempt to be subtle and always carefully watch for body-language indications of hurt, defensiveness or misunderstanding.

It Does Get Easier

Sometimes a seasoned pro can be airchecked in a single word. A good example is an aircheck session that KFI/Los Angeles news presenter Susanne Whatley had with her news director, Mark Austin Thomas.

Susanne recalls:

> He was trying to get me to 'brighten up' my performance. He gave me one word—"energy." Inside my own head I thought I was using enough energy, but when I tried it out his way, and then heard it back, my work sounded better! There is a lot of trust involved in doing what is suggested. When I first made the change, and pumped it up a little on the air, using higher energy, power, and pacing, it sounded silly to me inside my head, but when I heard it back on the tape, he was absolutely right.

There are additional methods that can help develop talent. Encourage talent to grow independently by trying new ideas, experimenting on the radio, and "self-checking," i.e., listening to tape on their own. You can also learn a lot from hearing others whose work you admire. You can even aircheck someone you have never met before, using tape you have made from the radio. It is a good way to see what qualities in their work are effective and might be adaptable to your individual performance.

Guy Zapoleon

Texas-based music radio consultant Guy Zapoleon "inspires hosts by playing a great talent example—past and present." Talent might wish to listen to a personality that they look up to in another market or, better still, someone who is on the staff who is philosophically aligned with him or her; and someone who can also be a mentor.

Airchecking looks easier than it actually is. Every coach has a different method.

Jaye Albright warns:

> Listening to your own work can be devastating. Seek objective feedback from as many directors as possible. Use what resonates truthfully with your own inner voice. Carefully consider the reactions of others, but do not ever take them personally. Their guidance is about their life experience and response to what you did. Try the things that seem sensible. Reject that which does not.

If there were an easier way, we would embrace it. Learning from others is something everyone does, but do not try to become someone else. Make it your goal to find your unique voice.

What Am I Looking For?

As I have mentioned, goal-setting is vital for successful airchecking. After all, the host needs to know, in a very concrete way, what is expected of him or her. Program director Alan Eisenson outlines three main qualities every show must have:

- **Always have at least one issue each and every hour you are on the air.**

Never go on the air without a specific agenda. Do not just meander and allow the callers to control your show. Always have something to say. Each hour must be relevant and substantive.

- **"Do I care?"**

Is the most important question. If you do not care about an issue, then you cannot make your listeners care. You cannot fake it, at least not long term. Your audience can smell an "act." Talk radio is not theater. You must always be real. Always tell the truth. Never fake passion, and never, never fake an opinion.

- **Once you've chosen your issue, focus it into a question that begs an answer.**

TV's *Ricki Lake Show* is an excellent example of framing topics into tightly focused questions. Although her actual issues do not come close to fitting the criteria for my radio station, the way she frames her issues into talkable topics is on target.

Getting It

Here are some real stories of ways in which talent recognized and overcame obstacles using aircheck sessions.

Aircheck Success Story #1
"You Big Meanie!"

Before her death, Mother Teresa was the subject of an hour's discussion. The host began the show by saying, "I think this religious figure, beloved by millions, is a fraud. I have an article in front of me documenting her luxurious lifestyle, the money she has been given, private jet travel, and other perks of celebrity. It says here she accepted a huge contribution that turned out to be from stolen funds, and then, when asked, refused to give the money back. After all that, she wants to be thought of as a saint?"

The host then took an hour of calls on what a bum he considered Mother Teresa to be. The following day, the program director was deluged with negative mail and angry calls. Much of the correspondence began by saying, "I usually love Dan's show but..." and ended with "I'll never listen to this radio station again!"

Why, the PD wondered, would this well-liked host generate such a heated reaction? The PD requested a tape of the show and found the problem immediately: Dan had only introduced his supporting data at the *beginning of the hour.* Listeners coming into the show after a break, without having heard the show's opening, would have no idea what motivated him to say such angry things. It sounded like he was picking on Mother Teresa for no reason at all.

It would have been possible to listen to an entire half hour of Dan's show and hear him and the callers going back and forth about the saintliness or depravity of a prominent religious icon without ever knowing the revelations and allegations of her worldly shortcomings.

Using the tape, the PD was able to explain to Dan that he had no problem with his opinion, however unpopular it might be. But he pointed out that Dan had not been *heard* or *understood* by a majority of his listeners, because he had not reset the topic on the air for the new audience tuning in. The host was so busy being angry and outraged, he forgot to mention periodically what had sparked his initial reaction. Dan had failed to explain again the *reasons* for his anger. The result: to a majority of his audience, he just sounded mean. With the aircheck tape and letters from people who usually liked his show, the host could clearly see the result of not resetting a topic: he had been misunderstood.

Resetting Your Topic

Resetting your topic at a minimum of every fifteen minutes is like giving your audience an on-ramp. Without resetting, it is like watching traffic on the freeway. You can see it go by, but you have no idea how to join in. Your show becomes accessible only to those who already got on the highway at the top of the hour.

Have you ever walked into a room where people were in the middle of a big fight were screaming at one another? You wouldn't want to be involved and would either avoid entering the room or leave as quickly as possible. But if they stopped fighting and someone said to you, in a reasonable tone of voice, "Wait a minute. She says don't eat that dessert, it will give me a heart attack, and I say enjoying my life is more important than living an extra ten years. What do you think?" You have now been invited in and may be willing to contribute your opinion.

As for Dan's show, the reset could have been done this quickly:

"I have an article that says Mother Teresa kept stolen money, demands first-class air travel, feather pillows in hotel rooms, and gourmet food on the road. I have lost all respect for her. Some of you are telling me: 'She is entitled to royal treatment for all the good work she does.' What do you think?"

Now the audience knows what is generating all that heat.
They might not agree with the host or the callers, but they have a handle on what is going on. It no longer seems like an unfounded nasty attack against a saintly old lady.

Aircheck Success Story #2
"What Happened to You?"

Rick had a weekend interview show covering serious issues. Around the station, he was charming, and funny. Rick told such wonderful jokes and stories, that management decided to give him a daily talk show of his own. It didn't work. Although his weekend show hadn't been a lighthearted affair, this new job was meant to be a smart, yet entertaining program. Unfortunately, every time Rick opened the microphone, he sounded stiff and authoritarian. Gone were the offhand anecdotes, the wry commentaries, and the relaxed original humor that everyone had enjoyed in the halls.

We scheduled an aircheck session with Rick. Something peculiar happened. Rick visibly bored himself. He skipped the tape over dull calls. He yawned, doodled on a scratch pad, and looked at his watch several times. At one point in the meeting, Rick actually dug around in his pocket for change and got up to buy a coke. Obviously if the host is bored with his own show, the listener is not likely to find it riveting entertainment.

There was another problem. Rick did not notice his attention was wandering.

This was the conversation:

PD: "Rick, what did you think of this tape?"
Rick: "It's OK, it's fine, this is how I do my show."
PD: "Rick, anyone who spends ten minutes in a room with you knows how funny you are. How come that's not on your tape?"

Eventually, we got our answer. It turned out that the reason Rick was holding back was because he was concerned about his reputation as a journalist in the community. He was afraid to have fun or loosen up on the radio for fear of not being taken seriously as an intellect. What would people think of him? He was worried he would lose his credibility, look foolish, or fail altogether.

At the end of the tape, there was a traffic report. The reporter got the hiccups in the middle of her segment. All of a sudden, Rick forgot he was on the radio. A simple body function brought out his natural humor, if only for a moment, as he suggested possible cures. We used those few seconds of tape to demonstrate to Rick how his spontaneity and storytelling humanized him and made him a more likeable air personality. We explained that that could be a powerful connection to an audience. Once Rick understood he could be the same person on the air as he was in the halls, he was able to make the change.

Aircheck Success Story #3
"Look Out the Window"

The sun was shining and flowers were blooming in Florida, and a weird weather phenomenon was taking place. During the night, strong winds from Africa had blown sand from the Sahara desert to area swamplands, absorbing the usual stifling humidity in the air. On that day, the weather was dry, warm, and clear, instead of Tampa Bay's usual unrelenting, sticky, tropical heat.

Blissfully unaware of the delightful spring afternoon in progress, the host on the air, a trained psychologist, broadcast two hours of carefully prepared and researched material on suicide and depression. The only people likely to have sat still for a show like that were probably incapable of physical movement. Great show. Wrong day.

During the aircheck session that followed, the host was very defensive. "I did everything I was supposed to," she said. "We had powerful stories from individuals involved in the experience, presented problems with solutions, painted word pictures. The show was personal without being too private, why are you on my case?"

"What did you do for the rest of the day after you got off the air?" I asked.
"Oh, it was such a wonderful day that I went sailing with my boyfriend, drank wine, had a picnic on our boat—it was bliss."
"Would you have listened to your own show out on the boat?" I asked her.
Silence.

It is always a good thing when programming, producing, or hosting a show, to literally take a look out the window and see what the day is like. It's part of what people are really thinking, doing, and talking about.

Aircheck Success Story #4
"Focus the Topic"

PD Alan Eisenson relates the following story:

> We had a talk host who found a great article in the Las Vegas paper. It was about a group of strippers bringing a class-action suit against a chain of strip joints for not paying them the minimum wage, while also taking a portion of their tips. The host read

> the short newspaper article, but he never really *focused* it into a *talkable topic*. The show turned into a meandering discussion of stripping in general and ended up digressing into handicapped accessibility on public busses. (I still don't know how that happened!)
>
> When we were airchecking, I asked the host if he thought this would have been a great show had he only focused the issue into a tightly framed talk-show topic, for example: Are strippers second-class citizens? Don't strippers deserve the same workplace rights as everybody else?
>
> It is the job of the program director to coach and direct talk talent and producers into thinking this way. Most good hosts and producers can smell a hot issue; the challenge is framing it into a talkable topic. When a host mentions a topic or issue, I always ask, "What is the point, or question?"

Sometimes it is not so easy to see the point or a question in an issue. Then you have to go deeper into the issue to find the talkable topic. Peel away the layers. It may take careful thought to get to the real heart of an issue.

Aircheck Success Story #5
"Did I Do That?"

Geller Media's Denise McIntee has the briefest but probably most common aircheck success story:

> I once played a tape of a host talking down and being curt to a lovely, articulate woman. The host was truly stunned when she heard herself and realized how bad it sounded. She never did it again.

Aircheck Success Story # 6
"Who Cares If You Don't?"

Here is another story from Alan Eisenson's files:

> I worked with a talk host who brought up the issue of drug testing. In listening to him, it became clear that he really did not care about the topic. Because he had no opinion about it, he had no story to tell. In that case, he never should have brought it up. He failed to engage the audience in the issue.

When this happens, the programmer should use the aircheck method and ask why the host chose his or her topic. If a show failed to engage the audience, the answer to this question tends to be something along the lines of "Well, it was on the front page, and I thought it would be good."

The PD should then ask some key questions, [*see pages 10-20 in the Personalities & Talent Section*], to determine if there was a reason the host cared, which he or she failed to mention.

If not, this aircheck session becomes an excellent opportunity to learn that you must, as Alan Eisenson says:

> Always have a strong opinion about what you are discussing. Do not ever do a topic when you do not have an opinion, unless you have a *guest* on the show who has a strong opinion.
>
> You engage the audience with your opinion/position or by telling a riveting relatable story about how the topic pertains to your life, or the lives of your audience. This is the *churn*, when your passion comes through and you can make your audience care about what you are saying. The show open or monologue is where you

set the stage for your entire segment. If you do not care about your subject, you will not find a way to engage your audience.

Feedback for Everyone

Programmer-turned-researcher Andy Beaubien warns that to neglect the talent may be just as dangerous and ineffective as bad airchecking. He recalls, "One person told me she made repeated attempts to arrange an interview with her newly appointed PD. After two months, she still had not succeeded. Various meetings had been planned, but the PD always cancelled them. Feeling totally ignored and undervalued, she quit the station and took an on-air job with a competitor."

Randy Lane knows a DJ who says, "If you aren't getting feedback or being managed properly to perform at your best, tell your PD or GM what motivates you and what demoralizes you."

Talent Respects Talent

Sometimes an air talent will walk away from an aircheck session feeling as though he or she has been stomped by a big boot.

KIRO/Seattle air personality Dave Ross has worked for several PDs. He admits he does not care to be critiqued in the traditional aircheck session. Understandably, he finds it difficult to be airchecked by someone whose judgment he does not respect. "I resent that it is just one person's opinion of my work. I much prefer to get up in front of a group of people at a live remote or performance and get instant, immediate feedback that way."

Former KFWB/Los Angeles news anchor Sheri Inglis believes in the process. "The most depressing thing you can do is slip a cassette of old work into the car tape deck and hear that you sounded better a couple of years ago when you were airchecked regularly. When I've been airchecked by someone who really knows how to do it, I give a better performance, and I can hear the difference on my tapes."

New Territory

The first time I airchecked a morning show, I was one of those nervous programmers. I thought, "Gee, who am I to tell these guys what is wrong with their show?" The night before I listened to hours of their work, made lists, took copious notes, and was too anxious to get much sleep.

After the next day's program, our three morning team members walked in, sat down, looked me in the eye, and waited for me to say something. With sweaty hands, I put the tape in the cassette player. Before I could open my mouth, one host said "No, no, no, let's skip over that part, wait until you hear the next part, now that was *funny*...and wait, back it up... here's where we had that boring caller! Wait, oh here I stepped on you guys and we screwed up the call letters, forget that...and here's the part where the caller started complaining about the prize because the dinner for two was at a restaurant that did not have free parking..."

This went on for about an hour and a half. I had not uttered a single word. At the end of the session, the guys stood up and smiled. "Valerie," one of them said, "you are great at this. It's the best aircheck session we've ever had."

These three broadcast professionals had known exactly what was right and what was wrong with their show. They just needed someone to be a visible audience for them and to witness their self-critique.

I learned more from those hosts than I taught them. This was my lesson: people already know their own strengths and weaknesses. All we as programmers and managers need to do is help them emphasize their strengths and conquer or play down their weaknesses. Our job, as Denise McIntee puts it, is to "work with the talent to examine what triggers the problem and aim to fix it."

Sometimes, as Massachusetts Institute of Technology Media Lab Professor Nicholas Negroponte says, "management can be measured in its quality by its perceived absence."

Valerie Geller's Key Principles of Airchecking

Our areas of weakness are probably the things we most dislike or avoid. That which comes easily to us is most likely our area of strength. This applies both to talent and management.

1) Define Objectives and Expectations

Outline to the talent what you look for in a show. Make very clear what you expect of them, and who the target audience is.

2) Do Not Lie

If the talent does not trust you or respect you, he or she will not listen to you. If something is not your favorite bit or moment, it can still have merit. Be clear about this.

3) Know Why the Show Is There

Remind yourself and the talent of the program's value to the station.

4) Provide Necessary Tools

Do not expect talent to make up for broken equipment, inept performances of others, or things beyond their control.

5) Ask More than You Tell

Find out why something was done before you react. As Randy Lane explains, "This sends a signal of respect for the personality rather than making an assumption or judgment before knowing all the facts. Interview talent as if you were writing an article on what makes their shows work."

6) Respect the Individual

Performers are not interchangeable talking meat. Do not force your talent to fit into a format or structure that is very wrong for him or her. Jaye Albright feels it is important to "come to aircheck sessions with the idea that I do not want to remake talent in my own image. It is impossible to get anyone to do anything he or she really does not want to do with any degree of commitment and conviction."

7) Preserve Privacy

Do not put copies of aircheck evaluations in the talent's personnel files. Nor should you discuss an aircheck session with others. Only tape a session if the talent wants to take the cassette and listen to it again later. For trust to develop, these sessions must be *private and confidential.*

8) Look for and Highlight Power Moments

What had you wanting more? As you listen to the aircheck tape, try to be aware of both your own comments on the air as well as those of others in your show. Remember, it does not always have to be *you* having the "power or magic moments," they just have to occur during your show.

Denise McIntee searches out these moments: "If a host is able to bring out a poignant story in a caller who was hesitant to tell his or her story, I point that out and *praise, praise, praise*."

9) Focus Only on the Show

This is not the time to take up other concerns. Tom Zarecki cautions: "Sometimes the aircheck session spins into a discussion of station issues the talent may be concerned about. Music, production, news, remotes, advertisers, other talent, may all end up woven into your aircheck chat. But keep them short. Just like the classroom full of kids who keep the substitute teacher distracted so he or she won't get to the lesson, make sure your talent isn't just trying to get you off the track."

10) Keep Egos Out

Talent, it is tempting to remind the PD that you are superstars in your market. Try to remember that your PD is really there to help you. Programmers, lower your ego shields. Be willing to listen to talent's ideas. Perhaps they resist your direction because they think it could work better another way. They might be right. Ask them what their ideas are. If they have feasible suggestions, throw out your ego and use them. Does it matter where a great idea comes from if it works?

11) Set Achievable Goals

As Lorna Ozmon puts it: "Avoid managing by minutia. When you focus on smaller sub-issues, you are perceived by the talent as 'picking on little stuff,' which they see as meaningless to their overall success. To recognize a big-picture issue, ask yourself, 'Will this behavior significantly affect the station's ratings or revenue?' If the answer is yes, it is a big-picture issue. Pick your battles. Fight for the big-picture issues, and let the talent win the minor skirmishes."

12) Acknowledge Accomplishment

Give authentic feedback for good work. Denise McIntee's strategy is this, "I do not use the session to point out 'faults,' but I might mention that when the host handled a similar situation in a different manner, it seemed to work much better. Ozmon says: "Most performers are 'pleasers.' When you tell them what pleases you, they will strive to do it again." Dan Vallie recommends following up meetings of substance with a memo to recap what was discussed. ABCNews.com's Vice President and General Manager, Bernard Gershon, stresses that you must "try to make it clear that the memo is a reminder for them, and for you—not 'evidence' to be kept on file so that you can fire them if they screw up again."

Choosing a Tape:

You are about to read the wisdom of several veteran aircheckers. Notice how different they can be. Once again, the "right" way to select tape for your aircheck session is the way that works for you.

There are several ways to do it.

1) **Neither the program director nor the talent has heard the tape before**. However, because it is advisable for the talent to select the tape, more than likely he or she has a pretty good idea of what is on it. Talent may have notes of problems or questions requiring a second opinion.

2) **The PD can receive a copy of the chosen tape before a session** and review it, making note of comments and questions he or she would like to go over with the talent.

3) **The PD selects tape** of a specific show. He or she may or may not choose to preview it. Often the reason for choosing a tape this way is that the PD heard the show live and noticed an area for discussion.

4) **Use a completely random selection.** For instance, send somebody back to the studio and pull any hour you can find. While at ABC Radio, then news director Bernard Gershon used this as a part of his development technique: "We had our on-air talent choose a favorite tape, then one of our managers selected a tape, and then one tape was picked at random. Usually, the talent critiqued the tapes first. Many times they were much harsher on themselves than you or I would ever be. They heard their inflections, imperfections."

How to Listen to the Tape

Note: The tape must *always* be available at the aircheck session.

Tom Zarecki suggests, "Listen to the tape and the person in front of you. The talent at some point will want to respond to you. Maybe not at first, but it won't take long."

Jaye Albright draws a distinction between someone you have worked with before and someone who is on a first "aircheck date" with you: "With new people whose styles I do not know, I begin by listening to a full, scoped half-hour of the show without comment. Then I solicit reactions to what we just heard to learn how they communicate, what they try to do on the air, how prepared they are, and what skills I need to focus on first."

Transcription

Consultant Lorna Ozmon favors sitting down with a cassette and transcribing a show word for word. Why?

> If you just listen back to the tape, sometimes the talent gets distracted by the sound of his or her own voice. If the words are written out, it works better. Listen to at least two hours of tape. Set time aside to focus on the show you intend to use for the aircheck. Do this away from other distractions, and make detailed notes. Look for patterns. If you have made good notes, you will begin to see one or two recurring areas for development.

I only use transcriptions when working in a language other than English, but Lorna has specific reasons for her method. She explains:

> Transcription provides talent with specific examples and depersonalizes the critique process. The 'script' is less threatening than "what I said." Don't pick out one bad break. Look for and transcribe breaks which show typical problems. This will deflect the impression that you are trying to find the talent doing something wrong and show that your intent is to help him or her.

Randy Lane favors transcription for slightly different reasons. He says:

Randy Lane

Experience the show as a listener. Listen to at least an hour of the show casually (like listeners) and get an overall feel for the show. Literally transcribe at least an hour of the tape or show while you listen. This enables you to be amazingly specific. Jot down the elements that you remember from the hour. This will give you an idea of what elements might be cutting through to listeners.

Keep Stopping the Tape

That is Tom Zarecki's method:

> Try this: Establish the tone of the entire meeting by rolling the tape for about 30 seconds, then stop. Talk about what you liked and didn't like about the way he or she introduced the hour. Click off the tape midsentence to compliment the talent on something specific. Nobody minds this. You can't do it too much.
>
> Nothing is more deadly and dull than pressing 'play' on the tape recorder, then the two of you sitting and listening to a few minutes of the tape, or even the whole tape without anybody saying anything.

Ask Questions

Whichever way you decide to work with the tape, here are some basic questions you can ask about the show. I would not recommend sitting with a checklist, but you might consider the following:

Did the talent feel the show worked? Did you? What parts were especially great? Was there anything here that could be used to promote upcoming shows? What bombed? Who was responsible? Was there a talkable topic or engaging question? Was the topic or question focused? Did it sound natural? Was the talent passionate about the topic?

Was it easily accessible to the audience? Was the talent nervous, unprepared, or anxious about the subject? Was the show accessible to people just tuning in?

Was There a Point?

Did the show fit the day? Were there any breaking news stories or other events that you should have covered but ignored?

Was the topic overdone? Did the talent feel pressured to work with a subject on the front page of the newspaper even though he or she secretly could not have cared less about it? Was it repetitious? Were there any other elements that would have encouraged tune-out? Was the talent trying to appeal to the emotion or humor of the listener? Scare or alarm them? Create anxiety? Simply entertain? Inspire, lift, or inform the audience?

Was the talent trying to persuade the listener to take a particular point of view? What are the tactics the talent used to attempt to capture the audience?

Were any mentally or visually intense images created? What drew the talent to this subject? Does the talent really care or have some kind of personal experience with this topic? Did the talent reveal those connections?

If he or she could turn back time and do the show over again, what would the talent do differently? How does the talent want to be perceived by the audience? Would a listener speak about things heard on your station tonight with a spouse at the dinner table?

About the Callers

How did the callers react? Were they informed, inspired, and entertained? Did they seem to know when you were kidding, when you were serious? Were they emotional? Were they articulate? Are you pleased with the length of each call? Do you feel you understood their points? Did they understand yours? Did they contribute anything to the topic? Did they add to the show's momentum, or drag it down? Did you feel like you were in control of the calls?

Did you change anybody's mind? Did anybody change your mind? Did any of the calls upset you? Make you laugh? Make you angry?

Were any of these callers a potential resource for a future show? If so, did your producer get their contact numbers? Were you pleased with the mix of opinions and the number of calls you took? Do you feel the same way about all of this right now as you did during the show itself?

Endear the *Listeners*

When people are answering questions about callers, it becomes obvious that some hosts resist confronting callers, even when their views are in contradiction. It is one thing to avoid confrontation between managers and hosts, but quite another to have a host who avoids it on the air. That is a sure way to a boring talk show. Tom Zarecki says, "Make the *listeners* like you, not the callers. Your greatest moments on the air may come from encounters with people who vehemently disagree with you."

It is up to the programmer to know how to ask questions and then listen to the talent's response. Manager and talent may not always agree, but a lot can be learned when these questions are selectively applied to a "bit" that is under discussion.

Room for Risk

Ultimately, because the PD usually wins in a fight to the finish, it is important to allow talent to make a genuine mistake without getting beaten up. Talent will make mistakes, but, reminds Andy Beaubien:

> Creativity cannot exist in a zero-risk environment. One of the PD's responsibilities is to encourage personalities to take calculated risks. Mistakes are a natural part of the creative process. That process involves dealing with unknown factors, the outcome of which is unpredictable. Conversely, making the same mistakes over and over again is not a sign of creative risk-taking but of carelessness and inattention.

If you want to show a talent what a bit could sound like if executed differently, you might try what consultant Guy Zapoleon calls the "before-and-after trick" of playing the tape and then playing an edited version.

Jaye Albright uses others' tapes to make her points:

> When airchecking, one approach I use that seems to have almost universal impact is to mix in tapes of other personalities showing how they handle the things we are working on. It's often possible to hear someone else make the same mistakes you do, and notice ways to correct those errors without defensiveness. It really helps to hear someone else successfully do the thing you are being asked to do.

Tom Zarecki's technique for listening includes these points:

1) **Have notes and take notes during the meeting.**
Have your own list of two or three points you want to cover. When the talent comments on something *you* need to handle (examples: unreasonable demands from a salesperson, uncooperative screener, equipment problem), write this down and take care of it. Let the talent see you taking notes on their comments. This prompts them to make more comments.

2) **Create a short, numbered "what-to-work-on" list.**
Your short list might be only one item! A typical list might say:

    A) Make opening remarks shorter. Get to guest quicker.
    B) Let callers provide the material. Don't be so quick to top them with your own lines.

3) **Make sure to date it.**

4) **Avoid the novel.**
Focus on the important things.

5) **Agree on concessions.**
You and the talent may each end up with your own short list of priority points to work on.

Tips for Teams

Here are some thoughts from a few top consultants on working with team shows; Tommy Kramer advises, "Team shows have some special needs. The objective is to avoid 'train wrecks', where the listener cannot tell what is going on." Here are his tips for teams:

- **Define roles.** The funny guy has to be the funny guy. To use a sports comparison, the play-by-play person and the color guy have separate, clearly distinct roles. Cast them as you would cast a movie, and then get the talents to stay in their roles. Nothing is worse than hearing two people try to top each other.

- **Listen to each other.** It is horrible to hear two people who each pay no attention to what the other says. How can they hope to connect with the listener? Tiny things can spur great moments on the air. But if the talent are not listening to each other, they will miss the cue.

- **Use hand signals.** Most teams think they do not need them. That is why so many teams talk all over each other. There is nothing compelling about hearing two people talking at once. Simply pointing at the other person right before your final word can correct this and make the sound seamless. It only takes a moment to point at the phone to signal that you are going to a caller or the CD player for music. Point at yourself to signal that you have something to say. Use the slit-the-throat signal to show "cut this off." Most teams get away from hand signals after a while, but if the timing gets off, go back to hand signals.

Tom Zarecki's thoughts on airchecking teams:

- The only thing you should not do in these team sessions is severely criticize any one person, especially the primary host.

- Most of any meeting with teams should be positive, upbeat, motivational. As in individual sessions, if something is great, react accordingly. Applaud. Play it again. Compliment specifics.

- Continue to meet with your primary host [and other team members] separately, to reap the benefits of confidential sessions.

- Before your meeting ends, make sure to set the date for the next aircheck session.

Finally, as Guy Zapoleon says, "Every great team needs to practice; you have to dribble before you can dunk."

It All Works Together

The aircheck process can actually help with show prep. Lorna Ozmon suggests closing the aircheck session with a discussion of new ideas. She says:

> "Look at the next month's calendar, and brainstorm for ways to capitalize on holidays or special events within the context of the talent's work on your radio station. Bring new books, magazines and newspaper articles which could serve as new sources of creative inspiration. Even if none of the ideas discussed are ever used on the air, this process helps keep the seeds of creativity alive."

Everybody's a Critic

Airchecking works best if there is only one person doing the feedback sessions. It can be very frustrating to hear comments from too many sources. The talent already gets feedback from his or her audience, producer, spouse, children, and people around the station. If you have clearly established your objectives and criteria for deciding what a good show is, adding the opinions and standards of others can only muddy the waters.

Don't Rely on Unreliable Feedback

The news director and staff of one of the most dreadful and lazy newsrooms I have ever seen felt no need to improve or change because they received the occasional fan letter. Remember, even the worst show has one listener.

Consider the talk host who opens the microphone and asks for comments on his or her show. Sure, there may be some helpful ideas generated, but if your goal is to increase your audience, the people you really need to ask are not listening at all. The feedback you are generating is not germane. If you ask the head of Elderhostel what he thinks of the big modern rock station in town, his comments may be heartfelt, but they are useless.

Untutored feedback sources can be deadly. I once worked with a station where the manager's wife was offended by a single remark on the station's morning show. As a result, the morning show was canned. That air talent walked across the street, got a job at the competition, and became number one in the market!

There is also a phenomenon where people may have a strong reaction to a personality and *say* they hate him or her, *but they listen everyday.* The same person who strongly claims not to like a show can often quote you chapter and verse what he hated on the air that morning, and the day before.

The moral here is this: powerful talent cause powerful reactions, both negative and positive. If your goal is to get ratings, understand what you are really hearing. Don't react to unreliable feedback.

One general manager actually fired a top talent because the complaint he received "was a particularly well-written letter and made an excellent case." Again, the talent simply packed up his huge audience and went over to the competition.

KFI/Los Angeles news-talk radio program director David G. Hall loves angry listener mail. On any given day, you can find the most vituperative letters tacked to his office door. You can hear the best irate phone calls by checking the station's web site. Complaints, boycotts, and protests can also be a source of great free publicity for your station, ultimately generating new listeners.

Where Is the Line?

With creative performers, there is a real danger of stepping over the line. Andy Beaubien points out that unreliable feedback can encourage talent to cater to an ever-decreasing segment of their audience:

> Content must be judged not only in terms of entertainment and information value but by legal and public taste standards as well. Many personalities constantly test these boundaries. The PD's job is to help personalities to stay within the necessary parameters without compromising the creative process.
>
> For obvious reasons, content that is offensive to the target audience or portions of it is to be avoided. Content that is acceptable to your target audience but not necessarily to the overall market may be permissible and even necessary.
>
> Personalities often find that certain kinds of "on-the-edge" material are very well received by a particular segment of their audience. In reality, that segment may represent only a small portion of the target audience. However, minority audience reinforcement can be very influential. If a personality is allowed to be swayed by this narrow audience segment, the overall cume will be reduced to an ever-shrinking core.
>
> This phenomenon is a silent killer. Because the active core can be quite vocal about its preferences, the departure of the greater cume can remain undetected until long after serious damage has taken place.

When you drive away your audience—that is the line.

Airchecker "To Do" List

1) Meet in a private area.

2) Turn off your phone and hang a do-not-disturb sign on your office door.

3) Allow one to two hours per session.

4) Have selected tape ready.

5) Have pad and paper for taking notes.

6) Have a calendar nearby to schedule the next regular aircheck session.

7) Sit together with the talent and listen to the tape.

8) Stop the tape often.

9) Always ask "why" before assuming you know, especially for things that did not work.

10) Make questions specific.

11) Praise all good work/power moments.

12) Set achievable goals.

Post Production Planning/Team Show

worksheet

Team Show Evaluation

The tape is not needed for this exercise.
Ask the team the following questions:

Guests:

Who is responsible for suggesting topics and guests?

____

____

____

Are you happy with the type and number of guests you use?

____

____

____

What would you like to change?

____

____

____

Post Production Planning/Team Show *(continued)*

Topics:

Who brings in ideas for the show?

____

____

____

____

Is everyone happy with this arrangement?

____

____

____

____

Do you feel you have/use enough sources for material? What other sources would you like?

____

____

____

worksheet

Post Production Planning/Team Show *(continued)*

worksheet

Promos:

Who is responsible for promos?

____

____

Are you doing the type and number of promos you would like?

____

____

What would you like to change?

____

____

____

____

____

____

____

____

Post Production Planning/Team Show *(continued)*

Nuts and Bolts:

Does your show get the technical support that you need? In studio? On remotes?

What would you like to change?

Does anyone keep a catalogue/library of past shows/bits/guests?

Can everyone who needs to access that catalogue/library?

Post Production Planning/Team Show *(continued)*

Worksheet

Personalities:

With which members of your team do you feel you should spend more time? Why?

____

____

____

With which people in management do you feel you need to spend more time? Why?

____

____

____

In your opinion, what is the one thing that would most improve your show?

____

____

Without adding more staff or equipment, how could you solve the above difficulty?

____

____

____

Post Production Planning/Self Check

Self-check Worksheet:

"I always wanted to be somebody, I should have been more specific."
—Lily Tomlin

1) Make a list of all the things that worked about the show.

____

____

____

2) Make a list of all the things that did not work about the show or that you did not like.

____

____

____

3) What could you have done to make the hour turn out better?

____

____

____

Go back and mark the points on the tape for the things that did not work.

____

____

Post Production Planning/Self Check *(continued)*

worksheet

Ask:

4) Was this my fault?

____

5) Why did it happen?

____

____

____

____

6) What was I trying to do?

____

____

____

____

7) Is this fixable? How?

____

____

____

____

Post Production Planning/Self Check *(continued)*

8) Did the topic have a clear focus?

____

9) Why did I choose this material?

____

____

____

10) How would a new listener understand this?

____

____

____

11) If not, what could I have done differently?

____

____

____

____

____

____

Post Production Planning/Self Check *(continued)*

12) Listening to this hour, did time seem to pass quickly or slowly?

13) At any time (be specific) did I entertain/amuse, inspire/move, inform, or give my audience an idea, material or something they could only have gotten from this show?

worksheet

Post Production Planning/PD and Talent

Evaluation for PD and Talent

Listen to the aircheck tape and then discuss the hour overall.

1) Does the talent feel the show worked? What were the magic or powerful moments in today's show?

____

____

____

____

2) Does the airchecker feel the show worked? What were the magic or powerful moments in today's show?

____

____

____

____

3) Was preparation adequate? Why or why not?

____

____

____

Post Production Planning/PD and Talent *(continued)*

4) How did the show sound? How could the sound of today's show be improved?

____

____

____

5) Was the talkable topic or engaging question focused? How could the topic have been better focused?

____

____

____

6) What was the point?

____

____

____

7) Why was this topic selected?

____

____

____

____

worksheet

Post Production Planning/PD and Talent *(continued)*

Worksheet

8) Were the listeners included, or would they have felt left out? Why?

9) Could a listener just tuning in understand this? If not, what could have been done differently?

10) Was the topic reset properly?

11) What was the worst moment? How could it be avoided next time?

Post Production Planning/PD and Talent *(continued)*

12) Was the talent prepared? If not, how could the talent have been better prepared?

____

____

____

13) How well were the formatics handled?

____

____

____

14) What risks were taken?

____

____

____

15) Were there any surprises? What were they?

____

____

____

worksheet

Post Production Planning/PD and Talent *(continued)*

Worksheet

16) Were the facts correct?

17) What did the listeners learn that would make them feel closer to the host?

18) What moments stood out, good or bad?

19) What were the powerful visuals?

Post Production Planning/PD and Talent *(continued)*

20) What was funny? Why did this humor work?

____

____

____

21) Is there anything you thought would be funny which did not turn out that way? Why?

____

____

____

22) What was emotionally moving?

____

____

____

23) Was there any new information for you? For your audience?

____

____

____

____

worksheet

Post Production Planning/PD and Talent *(continued)*

Worksheet

24) What was the best call you took? What did you like about it?

25) What was the worst call you took? What didn't you like about it?

26) Were you happy with the guest/expert, if any?

27) Was there anything about today's show that could become a promotion or ongoing topic for future shows?

Post Production Planning/PD and Talent *(continued)*

worksheet

28) Can you think of any way you could have covered this topic that might have worked better? How?

____

____

____

29) Was there any unique selling point, something that happened on your show that could not be found anywhere else? How will you promote it?

____

____

____

____

____

____

____

____

____

____

____

____

____

Post Production Planning/PD and Talent *(continued)*

Worksheet

Pick out one bit that worked and discuss the following:

1) One idea you will remember from the "bit"

____

____

____

____

2) One or more descriptive details you liked

____

____

____

____

3) Why do you think the bit was good?

____

____

____

____

Post Production Planning/PD and Talent *(continued)*

Setting Achievable Goals:

1) Identify what worked on the show. Talk about various ways the talent can continue to have those moments on the air.

____

____

____

____

2) Identify a problem, and offer a solution for the talent.

____

____

____

____

3) Pick a couple of "fixable" areas where the talent needs work. Write down one or two (at the most, three) goals that both the PD and the talent agree need attention:

____

____

____

____

worksheet

Post Production Planning

Worksheet

Example:

Show: John Claxton's Open Mic
Date: Feb 14 (aircheck tape from Feb. 13)
Time: 11:45
Place: Ed's office

Both John and Ed agree that
John's achievable goals this week include:

1)	Problem:	Ignored a potential issue raised by a caller
	Goal/Solution:	Listen more carefully to callers
2)	Problem:	Weak formatics - No call letters before commercials
	Goal/Solution:	Work on call letters - tape reminder note to console
3)	Problem:	Show opening is too long, slightly unfocused
	Goal/Solution:	Write down powerful topic point and use it first and last in monologue

Achievable goals:

1) Ignore distractions during interviews.
2) Keep working on those call letter mentions.
3) Work to tightly focus your show's opening.

Next Aircheck Session:

Date: Feb 21
Time: 12:30
Place: Lenny's Deli

Airchecking

Worksheet

Setting achievable goals:

Show: __________
Date: __________
Time: __________

1) Problem: ____

   Goal/Solution: ____________________________________

2) Problem: ____

   Goal/Solution: ____________________________________

3) Problem: ____

   Goal/Solution: ____________________________________

Achievable goals:

1) ____

2) ____

3) ____

Next aircheck session:

Date: __________
Time: __________
Place: __________

Post Production Planning

Guest/Caller Evaluation:

Host: ______________________________

Guest: ______________________________

Topic: ______________________________

Date: ______________________________

Instructions:

Listen carefully to the tape of the interview. Ask:

1) What demonstrates that you really listened to what your guest or caller had to say?

____

____

____

____

2) What demonstrates that your guest or caller listened to you?

____

____

____

____

Post Production Planning *(continued)*

3) How did you control the show/interview? How did you help keep the guest or caller on topic?

4) If you lost control, what could you have done differently?

worksheet

Post Production Planning/Guest-Caller *(continued)*

5) Are there things you would want to ask now that you did not think to ask then? What are they?

____

____

____

____

6) How were your comments on air useful/entertaining?

____

____

7) How did the guest inspire, make you laugh, entertain, or inform?

____

____

____

8) Would you like to have had the guest stay longer?

____

____

9) Would you like the guest to have left sooner?

____

____

Post Production Planning/Guest-Caller *(continued)*

10) How could you have accomplished either of the above?

____

____

____

11) Other thoughts on today's show:

____

____

____

____

____

____

____

____

____

____

____

____

____

____

Worksheet

How to Create a Powerful Audition Tape

"The great 'end' in life is not knowledge but action."
—T.H. Huxley

When Is It Time to Move On, Up, or Out?

As program directors and consultants worldwide have discovered, the most paralyzing thing you can say to an air talent is "Send me a tape..." Talent will agree to it, and then hem and haw and procrastinate. They hate making tapes. The general feeling is "I don't know what to put on my tape. I am the worst judge of my own work. How will I know what is good and what is garbage? What really represents *me*?" I once waited five years for an aircheck tape from a talent!

Here are some ideas and techniques to help hurry along those facing the excruciating dilemma of creating a demo tape.

1) **The aircheck tape should always leave the listener wanting more.**
The worst thing you can do is send too much tape. It's like overfeeding a fish until it dies. If you leave your audience just a little bit hungry, it will pique their interest in you. Your goal is to get the PD to ask for more tape.

2) **Don't get paralyzed deciding which tape to send.**
If you have an hour showcasing your versatility, send that. If you have a great hour showcasing only one aspect of your personality, send that. Then let *me* ask you for more tape. Most PDs look for talent who are equally good with humor, substantive issues, interviews, and breaking news.

3) **Show your heart**.
Show what you care about on your tape.

4) **Show your stuff.**
Showcase your technique. ABCNews.com's Bernard Gershon suggests: "If you are the person preparing that demo tape, put your best stuff up top—even a montage of some highlights—then more details. If you are weeding through tapes, listen for that spark—the edge that, with *your* guidance, will make that person a pro."

5) **This is your self-portrait on tape.**
This tape should be exactly as you want to be perceived by a potential employer. As KGO air personality Turi Ryder advises, "Make your demo or audition tape not for the job you currently have but for the job you *want* to have or the show you *want* to do. Keep in mind, the people listening to this tape want to hear not only what you have done, but also what you can do for *them*."

6) **There is nothing worse than being told that "you were never as good as your demo tape."**
As Ryder puts it, "It should be like a good, but not a rare, hour—one where you really do not want to edit anything out, but not as if a perfect human being with your voice was sitting in for you. I want whoever hires me from that tape to know what they are getting before I move my furniture."

On tape you can create a perfect self-portrait, but for your own good, make it an accurate one. Ryder warns music and talk hosts, "If in your typical day, a caller changes your mind or you must admit ignorance of which drug the murderer was on, or screw up the name of the Afghani foreign minister, than that is the show you do."

She points out the exception is in the case of news. There, an error-free tape is preferable.

7) **Showcase your most individual work.**
I like to hear shows that originate in people's lives. One example I use for coaching came from Swedish radio personality Jesse Wallin.

Jesse decided that he wasn't going to mix the formula for his new baby's bottle. He said it was easier to just spoon in the powder. That way, when the kid spit it up, all you'd need for cleaning would be a dustbuster or a vacuum. It takes a father who has cleaned up a lot of baby spit to think of that. I laughed, I was moved, and I cared about him.

8) **Think like a program director**.
Imagine your tape arriving in the mail. Now it is in the cassette machine, with an attentive, hopeful, and open-minded program director beginning to hear your work. Then the telephone rings. Ask yourself, would the PD stop your tape and get the phone, or allow someone else to answer it because he or she was too absorbed in hearing your work?

Looking for Talent

Make a tape that commands attention. Music radio consultant Guy Zapoleon puts it this way: "There is an 'X' factor. It is the feeling I get from listening to the talent."

What do *I* listen to? Everything that comes into my office. As Bernard Gershon says, "You have to review tapes, place ads, network, and listen to your competition in both smaller and larger markets. Try to find someone who you think 'gets it,' who has an original sound. If the person truly has potential, the rest can be learned."

What am I listening for? Anything that keeps me in a parked car in a dark garage with the groceries melting in the back seat, because I have to hear the rest of the show, is a keeper. If I cannot leave until I know what is going to happen next, you're in.

When listening to tape, music radio consultant Guy Zapoleon asks:

- Do they "connect" with the audience?
- Are there great phone calls where you get the feeling from the listener that they and the jock are truly friends?
- Are they creative at selling the radio station, using promotions, using liners?
- Do they still get excited by something that radio pros take for granted, but the listeners don't...the music?

Denise McIntee has sifted through New York City's radio applicants for seventeen years. Here is what she looks for in demo aircheck tapes:

> Do I laugh? First and foremost, I want to know if the host has a sense of humor. Do I want to keep on listening? Would I want this person as a friend? What did I learn from the host? Did I walk away from the show with a new perspective on a topic? Was the host able to persuade me to change my opinion? Is the host respectful to those who disagree? Can he or she "fight fairly" with a strong, intelligent caller?
>
> The host should have talent walking in the door. That is a given. But, *developing* energy, communication, and humor is tough. If a host does not possess these important vital traits, you should reexamine your hire. Very few people have it all. That is why there is a shortage of "genius-level" talk-show hosts and entertainers. Most times, "a leopard does not change his spots." If you start without the basics, you could end up stuck with a host you are constantly trying to change, rather than coach.

ABCNews.com chief Bernard Gershon has hired many news writers, anchors, and reporters. Most of what he wants in a candidate would be necessary qualities for anyone working on the air as well as for managers.

> When searching for talent at any level, I suggest looking for three primary qualities:
>
> - Intelligence
> - Desire
> - Sense of Humor

Intelligence does not just mean being book-smart or having a high IQ. Intelligence means the ability to solve problems; to complete complex tasks with resourcefulness, initiative, and resolve. A good job candidate also needs to be intuitive; to understand what is on listeners' minds, what will get them to tune in.

So, if you are interviewing potential talk-show hosts or newscasters, you need to find out what they are interested in, what stories push their buttons. Even if those story ideas sound boring to you, let *them* explain. They may win you over. That is what makes a talk host or newscaster great—the ability to communicate and excite.

An intelligent job candidate will also be looking for new challenges.
If you are interviewing someone who has seen it all, done it all, knows it all—move on. Curiosity is key to intelligence.

Do not be fooled by a long resume with important sounding titles and degrees.
I look for job candidates who have traveled, and have taken an eclectic mix of courses in college. I hold nothing against history or economics majors, as long as they have the ability to communicate.

Look for a sense of humor.
You are not looking for a wiseguy or a stand-up comic. But you are looking for someone who can roll with the punches, take criticism, and still take his or her job seriously. Someone who can relate well to fellow employees and diffuse difficult situations with humor and aplomb.

Getting a Job; The Tape Is Done. Now What?

You have made the perfect aircheck tape. It represents your best work. Your personality shines through. It is visual, informative, inspiring, funny, has tons of truth in it, and you know if you can just get it into the right hands, it will get you a job.

You will now learn one of the most disheartening lessons in radio: getting someone to listen to your tape is harder than you thought. Programmers, consultants, station group heads, and everyone else who can actually hire you are very busy men and women.

Jaye Albright explains, "It takes time to do justice to tapes people send. That is why I do not have time to do this sort of in-depth listening and thinking about more than one or two per day."

Talent is very sensitive. If a talent calls a programmer, sends a tape, calls again to follow up, but doesn't hear back, he or she is likely to get discouraged. My advice? Don't be.

Jock tapes tend to be three to five minutes long, and they arrive by the pound. Many of the people who send them have at least some experience, though not always. Talk tapes have to be longer—around thirty minutes. It takes longer to listen to them. Whatever the format, there are a lot of aircheck tapes waiting to be heard.

In talk radio, the number of tapes I receive from complete amateurs is staggering. The common rationale seems to be "Anyone can talk, right?"

Talk radio is an art, not a science. Finding those artists requires spending time sifting through the plethora of tapes mailed, handed out, or even dropped off at your door.

Here is how it happens for me: Typically, whenever I attend a talk-radio conference, I collect around fifty tapes in less than six hours—all personally handed to me by hopeful talent. When I return to my office in New York, there are dozens more waiting in my mailbox and my voice mail is filled with broadcasters asking, "Have you heard my tape yet? I sent it a month ago!"

When I walk in the door after three weeks on the road, jet-lagged, hungry, and exhausted, that is *not* the time you want me to hear your tape. Please cut consultants and PDs some slack. You want me to listen when I am "in the mood." And that mood is not on a reliable, methodical timetable. When I was an air talent, I never understood that things happened on *their* time, not mine.

Don't Rush Me

Programmers generally listen to tapes when they are in the market for talent. It would be nice if stations' needs always coincided with hosts' availabilities. Unfortunately, it seldom works that way. Sometimes PDs miss their chance at a great hire.

I once did a talent search where I listened to dozens of tapes I had stowed away, and found a young guy I really liked. I heard a lot of potential there. I called him in St. Louis, and he picked up the phone just as the moving van was arriving to pack up his stuff. He had accepted a job in Milwaukee two weeks before and was on his way. Although his tape had come to my office four months earlier, I hadn't gotten around to hearing it—my loss.

Do Not Develop "Attitude"

Unfortunately, when a programmer fails to respond promptly to an aircheck tape and resume, the talent can get really mad. Many lean towards the touchy side anyway. They take it personally. Some simply give up. If they are extremely annoyed at you, they could ruin great opportunities for themselves.

Talent may think: "I have called, written, e-mailed, and faxed. I put in a lot of work on that demo tape. My tape is good, and I want somebody to hear it and find me a job. Hire me, or at least tell me 'no.' It has been two months." Or, "What a jerk this guy turned out to be. He [or she] never even acknowledged receiving my tape. They couldn't pay me enough to work there now!"

In truth, it is entirely possible that the programmer has been busy, has not gotten around to hearing the tape yet, and does not want to call and say "no"—at least not yet.

However, if you call fifty times, you may get a "no" from a programmer just to get you off the phone. You can be sure if you become a pest, your tape has very little chance of being heard at all. Most PDs would interpret an overeager host as someone who would be a pain to have around the station if he or she were actually hired. The goal is to be politely persistent, not obnoxious.

Sometimes It Pays to Be Aggressive

Decades ago I went after a job I wanted very much. I knew the PD had offered it to someone else, but I wanted him to hear me before he committed to the hire. I called him up and played my aircheck tape for him *over the phone*. It was too late to get that job, but my tenacity impressed the programmer enough that he recommended me for other positions.

The Rules Change When the Program Director Solicits a Tape

It is not uncommon for a program director to get your name from a colleague, someone at a competing station in your market who listens to you, or through the grapevine. The PD or GM calls. You chat. It is very flattering. Things go well. You already have a job. You are not looking for work. It will take time out of a busy schedule to put together a tape, so ask some questions:

1) Are you simply curious about hearing what I'm doing, or do you have an opening coming up?

2) When will I hear from you after I send this tape?

3) Will you keep it confidential? I like my current job and do not want to start rumors that I am sending out tapes and looking for another gig.

4) If you truly need this tape immediately, may I have your Federal Express number? It is not unusual for a PD to solicit a tape and then let it sit on the desk for a while. If they need it that quickly, let them pay.

When To Send Out Your Tape

A logical time to start looking around for work is when you know people are hiring, unless you just want to make a connection for later. In the United States, it generally happens twice a year, like clockwork, just before the fall and the springtime Arbitron ratings periods. Not all the good jobs are advertised in the trades or want ads, so do some homework on your own.

If you know someone who has access to Arbitron numbers, get a look at the ratings for markets or stations where you would like to work. If you cannot access the station's numbers directly, check the Internet, contact the local newspaper's media reporter or use your ingenuity to obtain whatever specific information you can find. Search the radio websites. If you discover a daypart has had a bunch of down ratings books over a period of time, chances are the PD and consultant are thinking about making some changes.

"Sorry, Your Tape Is Garbage:" A Programmer's Horror Story

When I programmed WABC in New York, I was fairly organized about the hundreds of tapes that came in, especially because we had a well-publicized opening. It is my policy to listen to *everything*.

I had a system that included three big brown cardboard boxes. In the first box, which I kept on the floor by my desk, I had the "keeper tapes." Next to it was the second box, where I kept the "possibles" or people from whom I wanted to hear more tape. I kept the third, the box of "unlikely tapes," on top of my desk so that my assistant could write polite "no thank you" letters to those candidates.

Late one night, a new cleanup crew, thinking that the two boxes on the floor were trash, threw them away. I came in on Monday morning and looked around for the "good" tapes, but they were *gone*. Of course, the tapes in which we were not interested were still there, right on top of my desk.

It was humiliating to have to put an item in the trades saying, "If you sent a tape applying for our morning show, please resubmit it. The janitor threw it out."

On the other hand, if you really want to hear all about certain individuals, by all means put their tapes on top of your desk. It won't be long before you hear, "Oh I see Brian sent a tape... he's looking for work *again*?" Or "Is that

Sue Smith's tape? Her tapes sound great. Too bad she can never do a show to match them!" And here is the best comment I heard from a staffer who noticed a tape on her boss's desk: "Oh him... he's great on the air, but let me tell you about the time we had to bail him out of jail for drunk driving after he hit an old lady. Another time he showed up for work handcuffed to his date, and we had to hire a locksmith to get him out so he could do his shift..."

Heed this warning: Unless you truly want feedback from the staff on potential candidates, and do not mind if they go ballistic reacting to what is on your desk, do not leave tapes out for them to see.

If you are a talent who cannot risk having the world know you are looking to move on, when you send your tape, try saying, "I know some of your staffers. Whether or not you decide to hire me, I'd appreciate it if you kept my application under wraps." Most program directors will respect your confidentiality.

Finally, picture your tape in the programmer's office. Tapes go in one box, resumes in another. Be sure to fully label your tape with your contact number.

REMEMBER, tapes and anything else you send us get separated from their cover letters. WRITE YOUR DATA ON *EVERYTHING*!

Post Production Planning Notes:

Post Production Planning Notes:

Post Production Planning Notes:

The Powerful Radio Workbook:

Powerful News

The Powerful Radio Workbook:

Powerful News

"Storytelling is a basic part of every human culture — people have always had the need to participate emotionally in stories."
—Marlon Brando

News is very structured. Length, storytelling, relevance to the audience, writing, delivery, timing, authority, credibility, story selection, and use of tape are all verifiable. The other "X factors" of news are much the same as for other formats and discussed in other chapters.

Many of the points I collected for the news section were so universally applicable that they appear elsewhere in the book. However because news is quite specialized, and a vital part of talk and information radio, I have included my techniques, along with tips from some of the best in the business, designed expressly for airchecking news.

Get your facts straight.

This is the only way to establish long-term credibility.
When in doubt, leave it out.

- **Tell the truth**
- **Never be boring**
- **Make it matter**
- **Tell me a story**

The essence of news is the well-told story. If informative, entertaining, and up-to-the-moment, the story will always work.

I picked up the following ten point list years ago. I never knew who wrote it, but I carried it in my wallet, copied it for fellow broadcast journalists and friends, and used it all the years I worked in broadcast news.

1) **Create radio news with "ear appeal."**
Open your news with a sounder or great story to grab attention and set it apart from the other entertainment on the station.

2) **Call letters**.
Use them at the:
    - opening of the newscast
    - close of the newscast
    - going into the commercial
    - coming out of the commercial
    - in the sports segment
    - in the weather segment
    - within at least one story ("Mayor Grover tells KIOI News...")

3) **Ditch all wire copy.**
Rewrite every story in your own words. Tell the story—do not read the story. Rewrite multiple versions for ongoing stories so that they are *never boring*.

4) **Never start a story with a source.**
Phrases like "Police say..." or "Senator Joe Jones says..." or "The Red Cross reports..." make weak openers, because these guys say things all the time. It is *what* they say that is important, not who they are.

5) **Open with action words.**
Use powerful verbs that clearly tell immediately what the whole story is about.

6) **Keep actualities and sound bites short and colorful.**
Avoid using tape just for the sake of using tape. Remember, a good movie director leaves a lot of film on the cutting-room floor. Try to put only the great stuff on the radio. A rule of thumb is "one thought per actuality."

7) **NEVER put on a dull spokesperson.**
If you can say it better and quicker than a boring expert, do it.

8) **Commercial radio is a headline service.**
No matter what a newswriter thinks, a story becomes bulky and hard to digest after about three lines unless it is an ultra-hot breaking event. Research indicates listeners feel most satisfied when hearing a lot of items, rather than a lot of details on a few items. Try fitting in six to eight stories per newscast.

9) **Promote your newscast about ten minutes before it airs.**
Bring on the newscaster to deliver a couple of quick teases. In talk radio these can provide many magic moments. The best two stories to tease are usually the top story and the kicker.

10) **Don't sweat it.**
How long should it take to write a story? Usually if it takes too long to write, you don't "get" the story. If you understand the story, it should take about as long to tell it as it does to write it. Spend a couple of minutes writing each story. Try two or three sentences that say it all.

Basics

Double check to make sure all your news stories contain ALL of the following;

- **Who**
- **What**
- **Where**
- **Why**
- **When**
- **How** (how it happened, how it affects people, how much it costs, how it can be solved)

Always remember these points:

- Keep it conversational; write as you speak.
- Keep it short.
- Be aware of the listeners and who they are.
- Exercise good interview techniques.
- Prepare.
- Use your genuine curiosity.
- Ask anything.
- There are no stupid questions, so ask again if you do not get a satisfactory answer.
- Use the medium of sound.

Radio News Anchoring

Jerry Bell, news director of all of Clear Channel's Denver stations, including KOA, KTLK, and KHOW, could paper the walls of a mansion with the awards he has won for news excellence over the years. He calls his techniques, "The Zen Rules of News Anchoring:"

Jerry Bell

> Everyone wants to do the perfect, flawless newscast. That is a good goal, but a fear of making mistakes may end up being just the thing that keeps you from being a good news anchor. How? If you fear making a mistake you will never take a risk with your voice. You will be so uptight that you will constrict

your voice and cut off all the power and fullness that can come when you use your full vocal instrument. If you read every word individually, while being oh-so-careful, you will sound like a robot instead of a human being. You will be boring and lifeless on the air.

Jerry Bell's Zen Rules of News Anchoring

Background, Not Foreground

It is shocking for some talent to realize that the listeners do not sit with their hands cupped to their ears to make sure they are hearing everything you say on the radio. A good newscast demands your attention and must cut through the clutter of everyday life. Imagine your newscast as it is being heard on the car radio. Mom and Dad are driving their three screaming kids to school. At least three different conversations are going while the radio is on. What is going to come out of that speaker that will silence the crowd for even a few seconds? That is your challenge. *Guess what? Your audience is not hanging on your every word!*

To Err Is Human

Get your facts right, but cast off the nasty baggage that it is unacceptable to flub now and then in your on-air delivery. What is more important is taking risks and being able to put yourself out there without fear. The beauty of radio is that mistakes travel quickly to the void of outer space and are quickly forgotten. So you make a goof... no big deal. It is not the end of the world.

Radio Is a One-on-One Medium

If your news copy is written in a detached way and you speak *at* and not *to* your listener, you miss the essence of the medium. Radio is portable and personal. It travels with people. Aim your newscast at the individual, not the collective group.

What, Why, and How, Before Who and When (Most of the Time)

Good radio leads are not good newspaper leads. The newspaper gives you the old who, what, where, when, why, and how. In newspapers, the most important part of the story is where and when it happened. But in radio news, the more compelling radio leads usually deal with the effect the story has on the listener. Quite simply, how will the story affect you? What is the reason for it? Why is a change taking place?

Here is a good radio lead:

"Your taxes are about to go up."

That works better than:

"The State House voted last night to raise the property tax levy..."

Be a Person, Not a Newsperson

Read this lead:

"Police are beginning a probe into a probable homicide at 361 Elm Street. A 35 year old woman was found slain. The suspected murder weapon, a Colt 45 revolver was found next to the woman's corpse. Homicide detectives say the slaying has reported similarities to five other homicides in the neighborhood this year."

What is wrong with this lead? Everything. You have words no one ever uses in normal speech and it sounds so pompous as to be almost silly.

Instead, try this lead:

"A murder on Elm Street and the cops say the killer left his gun at the scene. Police are investigating the death of a 35 year old woman and think it may be the work of a serial killer. Five other murders in the neighborhood have the same M-O."

Sound Paints a Picture and Creates Energy

A good radio story should have sound that imprints pictures in the mind of a listener. You could read a story about a flood and get all the facts. But if you add the sound of the flowing water, a cry for help, the motor on a boat going down what used to be a highway, then you use our medium best.

Sound is not just sound effects. Most stories you hear on the radio have a tape bite somewhere in the middle. That is predictable and very dull. Clever news anchors will lead with sound or even use multiple tape bites to tell a story.

A Pause Refreshes

The small nuances of announcing separate the men from the boys and the women from the girls. Use a fraction-of-a-second pause for emphasis. The ever-so-slight elongation of a word will stress its importance. These are techniques used for centuries by the best orators in the world.

Take the *"I Have a Dream"* speech of Dr. Martin Luther King, and imagine how it would have sounded being read by a dull monotone news reader. The beauty of this speech is in the power of its words, the ups and downs. The elongation of key words, changes in volume, and the changes in pace give the speech motion and emotion.

These speech techniques, toned down a bit, can make your newscast come alive.

If It Were So Easy, There Would Be Tons of Great News Anchors

The sad fact is that most news anchors' airchecks sound exactly the same: dull and predictable. Here's why:

- Fear to go beyond the acceptable to reach the exceptional
- Lack of hard work
- Lack of coaching (or aircheck sessions)

Final Zen Notes

If you are learning this trade:

- Make aircheck tapes of your work, constantly.
- Send them to people you know and trust. Ask for and accept their harshest critiques.
- Acquire mentors who can coach you to greatness.
- Make daily airchecks, and listen back to your own work. Be your own worst critic.
- Becoming a good news anchor does not just happen. You have to work at it to make it happen.

Words Count

Deborah Potter

Everybody complains about bad writing. Deborah Potter, currently executive director of NewsLab in Washington DC, was a news reporter for years on CNN-TV and CBS-TV and radio. Potter maintains:

"Much of what we hear on the air is badly written. Guess what? The staff won't learn if no one teaches them. Good writing is not magic. It is a craft. It can be learned and it can be improved, but first everyone has to know that it matters."

Potter adds it is important to offer regular feedback about writing. "Words count. If you want listeners to tune in and believe what they hear, you need to care about what is being said. Praise good writing and you will get more of it."

Deborah Potter's "Write Stuff"

1) Take time at the front end to understand the story. Candy Crowley of CNN puts it this way: "The less time you have to write, the more time you should take to think about it." Try telling someone in six words or less what your story is about. If you can't, you will have trouble writing it.

2) Choose information that will tell the story best. Avoid the cramming impulse. Select specific details—the brand of beer, the make of the car—that will bring the story to life. Leave the rest out.

3) Organize your information in a logical way. If it helps, make an outline. Keep related facts together. Answer questions as they come up. Know where you are going before you start.

4) Tell it, don't report it. Imagine that every story you write begins, "Hey Mom, guess what I just found out!" Or, "Honey, you won't believe what happened today!"

5) Rewrite. Revise what you have written by looking at it backwards. Look closely at the end of every sentence, paragraph, and story. That is where you want the strongest words, because that is where they have the strongest impact. Crisp endings are one simple way to sharpen your writing.

6) Put your writing on a diet, and think of adjectives as empty calories. Particularly the adjectives so overused in broadcast news: senseless, horrible, tragic, ironic, and the like.

7) Do use active verbs that add energy to your writing. The right verbs do more than convey information. You build understanding and make the audience care. It's the difference between a story saying that a bus was involved in an accident and a story that tells how the bus skidded down an embankment, rammed into a guard rail, and flipped into a ravine. Active verbs in the active voice are the hallmark of writing that communicates clearly. The active voice tells you *who.* Then leave out all the words you do not need.

Where Have All the Writers Gone?

In an article published in the *RTNDA Communicator*, newswriting expert Mackie Morris, a TV consultant for Frank Magid & Associates in Dallas, laments the lack of excellence in the written word for broadcasting. He warns managers that it is up to them to encourage good broadcast newswriting: "The best writers I encounter are those who have something meaningful to say."

Mackie Morris

Mackie Morris' Suggestions:

- Require your people to read.
- Challenge them to think, and reward them when they write well.
- Establish a standard of good writing that applies to everyone in the newsroom.

Morris adds:

"Unless our newscasts begin to communicate in a more meaningful way, with clear and effective writing, we may not have any audience left. Our audience will have gone elsewhere for information and inspiration."

Mackie Morris first put out the *"Good Writer's Dazzlin' Dozen"* during his teaching years at the University of Missouri at Columbia, School of Journalism. The *"Dozen,"* is a great airchecking tool. It's a list of what to look for and how to do it right, for both radio newscasts and news reports. Even if you broadcast in a language other than English, there is still much usable wisdom here.

Mackie Morris' Dazzlin' Dozen:

1) **Write factually and accurately.** The best technique and the finest form mean nothing if the copy is wrong.

2) **Write in the active voice.** Your copy will be tighter, complete, easier to listen to and more interesting. Do whatever you must to avoid the passive voice (example: "He says" instead of "he said," "tells" instead of "told").

3) **Write in the present or present-perfect tenses.** They make your copy more immediate—and immediacy is more interesting.

4) **Keep your writing simple.** Write one thought to a sentence. Do not search for synonyms, since repetition is not a sin. Do not search for complicated intellectual language. Give the audience a better chance to understand the story.

5) **Be complete.** Make sure your quest for brevity and conciseness does not cause you to omit necessary information.

6) **Be creative.** Stick to the rules, but develop your own style. Try to say the same old thing in a new way. Make use of the "rule of threes" ("Lions and tigers and bears, oh my!" or, "Life, liberty and the pursuit of happiness...") and other effective writing devices that cause copy to be more interesting.

7) **Write to be heard.** Maintain a sense of rhythm in your writing. All life has rhythm, and rhythmic writing is easier to hear. Be careful of confusing homonyms. Always, always test your broadcast copy by reading it aloud.

8) **Avoid interruptives.** Do not force the listener to make difficult mental connections. Put modifiers next to what they modify. Do not split verb phrases.

9) **Avoid commas.** A comma demands a hitch in your reading and the result is a jerkiness that frustrates the listener. Avoiding commas also will eliminate awkward subordinate clauses. Such clauses kill the impact of copy especially if they come at the top of a story or sentence. Only put a comma where you intend to pause.

10) **Avoid numbers.** The listener has trouble remembering them. Instead of "48% of a population consisting of nearly 987 thousand people," try, "About half the population of nearly a million..." It is easier to "see" and remember.

11) **Avoid pronouns.** If you must use a pronoun, make sure it agrees with its antecedent.

12) **Create word pictures** so the audience can "see it." Use the medium of imagination.

For more expert advice on excellence in news writing, I highly recommend Mervin Block's *Writing Broadcast News, Shorter, Sharper, Faster.* My favorite Block quote: "Write to express, not to impress."

Building a Great News Team

Bernard Gershon is the Vice President/General Manager of ABCNews.com and former news director of ABC Radio.

Here are some of the traits he looks for in a newsperson:

Desire or hunger is crucial

The best employees always want to improve their performances. They display this by asking for additional assignments, wanting to learn different parts of the business, asking to be sent to training seminars. They also understand that getting better requires hard work and long hours. Look for people who are aggressive when it comes to getting interviews, going after callers, going "prime time."

Bernard Gershon

What we look for

An effective newsperson exudes "energy." To me it means someone who can generate enthusiasm and excitement from listeners—someone who is interested in the topic, the caller, the JOB. My definition of dull? Demo tapes of newscasters who sound like they are reading. Those tapes can be identified in about 30 seconds … then go in the trash can. Yes, it is a cruel business, but everyone is busy.

Warning: I have seen far too many job candidates who expect to become radio or TV stars—or both—overnight. These people are usually too egotistical to understand that they have to work as a team, pay their dues and gain a reputation. My suggestion ... pass!

The following pages are worksheets designed for you to help write, focus and create Powerful Radio News. Just as a pilot does his or her checklist before taking off in an airplane, make sure to double check your list before you go on air. Avoid the "disaster" of incomplete stories or items without purpose or focus that are boring.

Powerful News

Worksheet

1) What is the subject? ________________________________

____

____

2) How will this matter to our audience? ________________________________

____

____

____

3) Does this affect the health, human emotions, money, safety or other concerns of our listeners? How? ________________________________

____

____

____

4) Go global. How big can the story be? Can a huge national or international story be told with a local angle? If so how?________________

____

____

____

Powerful News *(continued)*

5) Think Local. How small (local or personal) can this national or international story become? ______________________________

____

____

Example:

> "One hundred million dollars is the amount that Best Oil Company will have to pay for cleanup of the largest toxic spill ever to hit the American Southwest. But right here in Franklyn, the Environmental Protection Agency reports some dangerous pesticides leaking into our own groundwater. The cost of cleaning that up will be high."

Is there a second day or "Monday angle" for this story?

____

If there are several angles to the story, can multiple versions be made?

____

Make sure the story contains everything important. Double check it. When you are pressured or in a hurry it is easy to leave out one or more important elements.

worksheet

Powerful News *(continued)*

worksheet

Ask:

1) Who is the who? ______________________________

____

2) What is the what?______________________________

____

3) Where is the where? ______________________________

____

4) When is the when? ______________________________

____

5) Why is the why? ______________________________

____

6) How? (How much it costs? How it affects people? How could this happen? etc.) ______________________________

____

____

____

Powerful News *(continued)*

Worksheet

Then:

1) Write the lead. ______________________________

____

2) Rewrite the lead (for future versions). ______________________________

____

3) Write the story. ______________________________

____

____

____

____

____

____

____

____

Powerful News *(continued)*

4) Now go back and find the most powerful line in the body of your story to engage the listener. Make it your lead sentence.

Use the word "you" to engage listeners immediately.

5) If you ask a question or present a problem, also try to present a solution.

Example:

For the past two months it appears several City Hall employees have been filling their gas tanks, ordering unneeded supplies and eating out at five star restaurants at the tax payers' expense. How could this happen? According to Mayor Stone Wall, *"No one has been in charge of the money or monitoring new expenditures since the city auditor left. I've been waiting for my replacement candidate to be confirmed."* These charges of corruption should speed up that process.

Powerful News Notes:

Powerful News Notes:

Powerful News Notes:

The Powerful Radio Workbook:

Powerful Promos

The Powerful Radio Workbook:

Powerful Promos

"The ability to communicate color, content and drama of an upcoming radio episode in a thirty second promo is rare and glorious. Talented promo writers and producers are the alchemists of our industry."
—Doug Harris
Promotions Consultant (Creative Animal)

Up Next—Powerful Anticipation

One of the most highly paid positions at a major market radio station is that of production director. Radio stations are not known for throwing money around needlessly, so there must be something rare and special about a nonmanagerial position that can command almost as much salary as is spent on a morning show.

Creativity is the "X factor" that makes the production director such a valuable member of the team. One nationally known production director says, "Your product is the station's package. Your promos are the wrapping paper and the bow on that package. Having great promos makes the listener want to open up the box and see what's inside."

Create Expectations

Innovatively produced promos for your station and your shows make the audience feel they will miss something if they tune away.

Maybe, a listener is not interested in whatever is on the air at the moment. However, if you can create excitement and anticipation about an upcoming event, the listener may give you five or ten extra minutes of his or her time, or come back later.

Pick the Highlights

Promos can establish your station's "personality," or image. Some call it "stationality." You know you have a great station when you have trouble deciding which moments to promote.

Station promos are a lot like movie promos. They incorporate peak experiences and show highlights to create excitement, energy, and, most of all, the desire to "be there." Like many movie trailers, the promos may often be better than the shows themselves.

Seize Opportunities

Anything from an upcoming appearance to the top-of-the-hour ID can become an opportunity to creatively promote your station. There's just one rule: if it is on tape, it has to be perfect. Make sure you have a good-quality aircheck tape or a digital recording of your station in order not to miss the chance to use a "magic moment" for a show promo. You may come across some of these moments during aircheck sessions, and it is very frustrating when the tape is of quality too poor to use for a produced promo.

You do not need to have a huge budget to run great promos on your radio station. If you have creative air talent, you can harness their abilities to promote not only their own shows but the station itself.

If you have access to the internet, you may wish to listen to some of the hundreds of audio feeds from various stations' web sites. There, you will find a mix of hot promos, parody songs, and creative spots. In addition, many production directors maintain their own web sites featuring examples of their best work.

Remember, when you make your promos, formatics count. Don't miss an opportunity to give call letters, dial position, and the station's name.

▼

Promo Points: News/Talk Radio

Teases and Promos Are Best When Short

If you err, err on the side of brevity. It is better to leave the audience hungry than to overfeed them.

Cross-Promote Like You Mean It

Having each host enthusiastically mention other shows and events on the station promotes and personalizes both the hosts and the station. There is nothing like a word of endorsement from a listener's favorite host to make that listener give another show a chance. If you are not a particular fan of the show you are being asked to promote, find one or two genuinely good things you *can* say, and say them. For example, "Sam's show got rated number one in the Reader's Choice Poll of City Magazine!" You don't have to lie, you just have to realize that when someone on your team succeeds, you win too.

If you are the number one show on the number seven station, it is not nearly as rewarding as being the number one host on the number one station.

Many of the biggest syndicated hosts in America take the time to cross-promote others on their local stations and their affiliates as well. Cross-promotion gives your schedule a feeling of continuity.

Throw Out Stale Bread

It is tempting to use great promos over and over again. I've heard stations use the same old promos for days, weeks, even years. Do not give in to that temptation!

Even if you have produced the most hilarious promo—distinctive, memorable, and featuring seven of the biggest stars in Hollywood—after a while, it gets boring. In fact, if a listener hears the same promo over and over again for weeks, he or she may deliberately avoid a show, associating it with a boring or annoying promo. If a promo is really that fantastic, run it for a little while, store it for several months, and then recycle it.

Keep a library of stand-out promos that are not date-specific in the event you are unable to produce a fresh one for some reason.

Change your promos like you change your underwear. If someone complains and says, "But I did one last week and it's good enough," remind him or her that creativity leads to more creativity.

Stay "Up" For It

If you cut your promos last thing before you leave the station, there is a danger of sounding tired and unenthusiastic. After all, you have just spent three hours on the air, you want to go home, and you are holding your car keys. Try running into the production room *prior* to today's show and see what you can come up with to promote tomorrow's show. The promos will have that sound you have when you first go on the air—spirited and full of energy.

Get It Right

When you work with prerecorded elements, *make them perfect.* Live on the air, you cannot possibly control everything that happens. But with tape, you can. Make it flawless. Working with tape, you can create radio art.

Creating Powerful Promos:

You can creatively "promo" anything. No matter how boring the subject, the promo should never be boring. The purpose of the promo is to entice the listener to come back later and hear what you've got.

Here is an example of a radio station bragging about its new, increased transmitter power on the air. The station, KGO in San Francisco, had undergone a costly power upgrade, and wanted to let its listeners know. Tom Bodett, a popular author, broadcaster, and spokesperson for the Motel 6™ hotel chain in America, did the spot. Bodett is famous for the tag line: "We'll leave the light on for you." Here's the actual KGO promo:

> *Soft country-style music plays behind the spot.*
>
> "When a radio station has been around as long as KGO, some of that electronic stuff's bound to wear out. Well, since it did and not everyone can talk real loud like that Ronn Owens or Bernie Ward, KGO went and got one of those new gillion-watt transmitters to squirt those sound waves out there." *(electrical sizzling sound effects)*
>
> "Well, sure, it's a big deal to the baby harp seals up in Nova Scotia that are now getting a fuzzy earful of KGO at night, but what's it mean to you?"
>
> "Well, not much except you might not need to use that microwave to heat your Lean Cuisine anymore and you probably won't have to actually switch on the lights either. Just turn on KGO and stand back..."
>
> "I'm Tom Bodett, and we've cranked up the power for you on KGO News/Talk 810."

To write, produce, and create powerful promos, begin by thinking of how *you* could be enticed to tune in. A great promo will intrigue the audience with a promise of something interesting coming up. They will be disappointed should the actual item not stand up to the promo. (In fact, the research on TV news promos indicates that some TV stations promote a bit *too* well.) You will quickly lose credibility as well as listeners if you only sell the "sizzle" but have no steak.

There are various styles of promos. If you want to experiment with your station's image and build continuity between shows, try to create the image that the radio station is like a family and all the hosts listen to and support one another. When done well, it really works. The "inside" promo is the method of one host promoting his or her show within another host's show. Your talkable topic or engaging question can make a good promo, as well.

Sample Promo:

> "Hi, I'm Sam on WKXW, AM 810, The Talk Station. Right now you are listening to the Dr. Paula Show, but I'd like to invite you to join me later on this afternoon. We'll be taking calls, the mayor will check in, and you'll get a chance to meet Elizabeth Taylor. That's today at 2:00 here on the Talk Station."

Listen to your station's other programs. Then you'll really know the product you are promoting.

Promos

Formula for Direct Promos

Example:

> "In ten minutes on WWXX, you'll meet the man who saved California's gray whales, and later in the show, Joe Jones' lawyer. He's defending the notorious artist, internet celebrity, and death-row inmate. On AM 680, WWXX."

Promo (15 seconds)

1) Host ______________________________

____

2) Station ______________________________

3) Time coming up (next hour, later today...) ______________

____

4) Teaser ______________________________

____

____

5) Call letters ______________________________

Promos

Select a single hour of an aircheck tape.

Make three separate promos using any of the following:

1) A highlight of a meaningful moment

____

____

____

____

2) A "bizarre" moment

____

____

____

____

3) A moment in which you sounded funny

____

____

____

____

Promos *(continued)*

worksheet

4) **A moment in which a caller/guest was funny**

____

____

____

5) **A moment in which you and the caller disagreed**

____

____

____

6) **A moment in which you were angry**

____

____

____

7) **A promo with a "wraparound voice-over" with a montage of sound pieces you have collected from the show**

____

____

____

Experiment to see what will work best. Try doing your promo with music but no sound effects, or using sound effects and no music.

Promos/Parody Songs

worksheet

Creating the Powerful Parody:

Promos and parody songs can be a powerful way of getting a message across in a unique manner. If you're musically creative and you like to sing, this may be a method that works for you. Parody songs can also be used as show prep to get your point across in a fun way. Here's how to create a powerful parody song:

Pick a current event, news story, or a celebrity *you* find humorous—then do one of the following:

A) Pick a song that has a "hook" close to your topic.

B) Pick a very popular current tune that is easy to sing.

C) Use a nursery rhyme.

Note: *The Green Book of Songs* by Jeff Green has song titles listed by topics—it is great for parody songs. You can also obtain "karaoke" style CDs. With only the music bed; they are easy to write and sing with.

Promos/Parody Songs *(continued)*

Worksheet

ORIGINAL LYRICS

YOUR LYRICS

Roll the tape and sing sing sing! (Not too loud.)

Powerful Promos

Notes:

The Powerful Radio Workbook:

Final Notes

The Powerful Radio Workbook:

Final Notes

"Before the beginning of great brilliance, there must be chaos.
Before a brilliant person begins something great, he must look foolish to the crowd."
—i ching

Airchecking really works. For years, I worked hard at a series of radio stations around the country, constantly packing up boxes and moving on to the next better job. In a way, it was like a journey without a map. I enjoyed the successes that I had, but I always felt alone in my work, with no one to offer me constructive criticism and actual techniques to improve my on-air performance.

I probably could have avoided several failures if I had had a set of tools for growing, along with someone to help me learn to use them.

When I started Geller Media International, I made up my mind that if I could do one thing, I would attempt to work with talent and highly creative people in a way that would support them. They would feel safe enough to climb to the next level.

When most people hear the words: "We are bringing in a consultant and we want you to meet with him (or her)," they get scared and think, "This means I'm awful and they want to fire me."

It does not have to be that way. If just one manager and one talent can sit down, work with this aircheck material and improve their show, I will have succeeded with this book.

Everyone is capable of moments of brilliance. My job is to help make those moments more plentiful.

This *Workbook* offers methods and techniques which have been successful for many winning broadcasters. However, the real work is not just reading this book, but in applying the "Creating Powerful Radio" principles daily in prep, performance, and aircheck sessions.

Without proper coaching, encouragement, and a conducive station environment, many talented people become discouraged and simply give up. Powerful radio takes persistence.

If being a broadcast communicator is something you *know* you have to do, keep at it. As actress Mary Pickford once said: "Supposing you have tried and failed again and again. You may have a fresh start any moment you choose, for this thing that we call failure is not the falling down, but the staying down."

It is not by chance or accident when a talent has a huge following. To be effective and powerful on the radio, day after day, takes hard work, support, skill, training, a tenacious spirit, and an artist's soul.

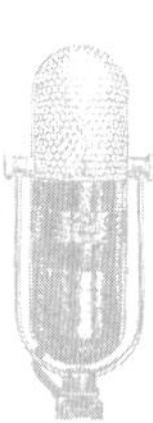

If you would like further information on
Geller Media International™ or the
Creating Powerful Radio™ workshops or
The Producer's Workshop
contact:

Geller Media International
666 West End Avenue
Suite 11-M
New York, NY 10025

phone +1-212-580-3385
fax +1-212-787-6279

email Vgeller@aol.com
internet http://www.gellermedia.com

Resources

Workbook Contributors:

JAYE ALBRIGHT
President
Country Programming
McVay Media
7699 Fletcher Bay Rd., NE,
Bainbridge Island, WA 98110-9200
Phone: +1 206 498-6261
Fax: +1 206 780-9200
e-mail: albright@usa.net

ANDY BEAUBIEN
European Operations Manager
Broadcast Programming & Research
European address:
22 Rue Crillon
69006 Lyon, France
Phone/Fax: +33 4 78 94 33 59
e-mail: andybpr@compuserve.com

JERRY BELL
News Director-Clear Channel
KOA-AM KTLK-AM Radio
4695 S. Monaco St.
Denver, CO 80237
Phone: +1 303 713-8000
Fax: +1 303 713-8735
e-mail: JBell@clearchannel.com

SUSAN BERKLEY
Berkley Productions
616 Palisades Ave.
Englewood Cliffs, NJ 07632
Phone: +1 800 333-8108
Phone: +1 201 541-8595
Fax: +1 201 541-8608
e-mail: infome@greatvoice.com.
(for online newsletter)
Internet: www.greatvoice.com
Speak to Influence: How to Unlock the Hidden Power in Your Voice

ALAN EISENSON
Program Director
WEVD-AM
333 7th Ave. 14th Floor
New York, NY 10001
Phone: +1 212 760-1050
Fax: +1 212 239-7203
e-mail: aceisen@aol.com

BERNARD GERSHON
Vice President/General Manager
ABCNews.com
77 West 66th street, 3rd floor
New York, NY 10023
Phone: +1 212 456-2222
e-mail: Bernard.L.Gershon@abcnews.com
Internet: http://www.abcnews.com

TOMMY KRAMER
Market Talent Coach
Clear Channel, Dallas
12123 Inwood Circle
Dallas, TX 75244
Phone: +1 972 770-7732
Fax: +1 972 385-1211
e-mail: tommykramer@att.net
Tommy Kramer's *"Coaching Handbook"*

RANDY LANE
The Randy Lane Co.
860 Via De La Paz Suite D2
Pacific Palisades, CA 90271
Phone: +1 310 454-4206
Fax: +1 310 454-5046
e-mail: enalydnar@aol.com

DENISE McINTEE
Broadcast Consultant
Geller Media International
666 West End Ave. Suite 11-M
New York, NY 10025
Phone: +1-212-580-3385
Fax: +1-212-7876279
e-mail: denisemac1@aol.com
Internet: www.gellermedia.com

MACKIE MORRIS
Vice President
The Magid Institute
PO Box 866576
Plano, TX 75086-6576
Phone: +1 972 403-7133
Fax: +1 972 473-2333
e-mail: mackie.morris@magid.com
Internet: www.magid.com

TONY NOVIA
Contemporary Hit Radio
Editor Radio & Records
10100 Santa Monica Blvd.
Los Angeles, CA 90069
Phone: +1 310 553-4330
Fax: +1 310 203-9763
e-mail: tnovia@rronline.com
Internet: www.rronline.com

BOBBY OCEAN
Bobby Ocean Inc.
Professional Creative Services
224 Blackstone Dr.
San Rafael, CA 94903
Phone: +1 415 472-5625
Demo: +1 415 472-7045
Fax: +1 415 472-1686
e-mail: oceanvox@pacbell.com
Internet: www.bobbyocean.com

LORNA OZMON
Ozmon Media
1123 W. Columbia Ave.
Chicago, IL 60626
Phone: +1 773 761-0305
Fax: +1 773 761-4490
e-mail: lozmon@aol.com

DEBORAH POTTER
Executive Director
Newslab - A TV News Laboratory
1900 M St. NW Suite 210
Washington, DC 20036-3530
Phone: +1 202 969-2536
Fax: +1 202 969-2543
e-mail: potter@newslab.org
Internet: www.newslab.org

HOWARD PRICE
Eyewitness News - WABC-TV
7 Lincoln Square
New York, NY 10023
Phone: +1 212 456-3173
Fax: +1 718 281-2172
e-mail: HBPrice@aol.com
Internet: www.7online.com

DAN VALLIE
Vallie-Richards Consulting
PO Box 1065
Blowing Rock, NC 28605
Phone: +1 828 262-3919
Fax: +1 828 262-1754
e-mail: Valirich@aol.com
danvallie@aol.com
Vallie-Richards publishes
"Radio Focus" - Monthly
$120/Year, $65 Half Year

TURI RYDER
PO Box 20045
Piedmont, CA 94620

GUY ZAPOLEON
Zapoleon Media Strategies
4800 Sugar Grove Blvd., Suite 170
Stafford, TX 77477
Phone: +1 281 980-3665
Fax: +1 281 980-3708
e-mail: gzapoleon@aol.com
Internet: www.zapoleon.com

TOM ZARECKI
Radio Computing Services
12 Water Street
White Plains, NY 10601
Phone: +1 914 428-4600 ext. 143
Fax: +1 914 428-5922
e-mail: tomz@rcsworks.com
Internet: www.rcsworks.com

Index

Index

Index

Index

Notes

Notes

Notes

Notes

Notes

Notes

Notes

Notes

Notes

Notes

Notes

Notes

Order Form

Order additional copies of **THE POWERFUL RADIO WORKBOOK** *or* Place an order for ***Creating Powerful Radio,*** A Communicator's Handbook

❑ **Please send _______ copies of THE POWERFUL RADIO WORKBOOK** U.S. **$39.95** *(plus S&H)*

❑ Please send _______ copies of ***Creating Powerful Radio*** U.S. **$24.95** *(plus S&H)*

NAME ______________________________

COMPANY ______________________________

ADDRESS ______________________________

____

CITY ______________________________ STATE ______________________________

ZIP/ POSTAL CODE ______________________________ COUNTRY ______________________________

TELEPHONE ______________________________

FAX ______________________________ E-MAIL ______________________________

Shipping and Handling

U.S.	$5.00 per book (Priority Mail).
Canada and all others	Call for the latest rates (Air Mail).

Payment

All forms of payment must be in U.S. funds. No COD's please. Discounts are available for educational institutions and multiple-copy orders. Call for more information.

❑ Visa ❑ Mastercard ❑ American Express

❑ Check (U.S. only) ❑ Money Order (U.S. Bank)

Card number ______________________________ Exp. date ______________________________

Total amount ______________________________

Name as it appears on the card ______________________________

Billing address (Amex only) ______________________________

Signature ______________________________

Fax orders:	**+1-615-251-8798**
Phone orders:	Toll-free **1-800-248-4242**; Outside the U.S., call +**1-615-251-1525**.
Mail orders:	**M Street Publications** **54 Music Square East, Suite 201** **Nashville, TN 37203 USA**

M Street PUBLICATIONS

Order Form

Order additional copies of **THE POWERFUL RADIO WORKBOOK** *or* Place an order for ***Creating Powerful Radio,*** A Communicator's Handbook

❑ **Please send ______ copies of THE POWERFUL RADIO WORKBOOK** U.S. **$39.95** *(plus S&H)*

❑ Please send ______ copies of ***Creating Powerful Radio*** U.S. **$24.95** *(plus S&H)*

NAME ____

COMPANY ____

ADDRESS ____

____

CITY ____________________ STATE ____________________

ZIP/ POSTAL CODE ____________________ COUNTRY ____________________

TELEPHONE ____

FAX ____________________ E-MAIL ____________________

Shipping and Handling

U.S.	$5.00 per book (Priority Mail).
Canada and all others	Call for the latest rates (Air Mail).

Payment

All forms of payment must be in U.S. funds. No COD's please. Discounts are available for educational institutions and multiple-copy orders. Call for more information.

❑ Visa ❑ Mastercard ❑ American Express

❑ Check (U.S. only) ❑ Money Order (U.S. Bank)

Card number ____________________ Exp. date __________

Total amount ____________________

Name as it appears on the card ____________________

Billing address (Amex only) ____________________

Signature ____________________

Fax orders: **+1-615-251-8798**

Phone orders: Toll-free **1-800-248-4242**; Outside the U.S., call +**1-615-251-1525**.

Mail orders: **M Street Publications**
54 Music Square East, Suite 201
Nashville, TN 37203 USA

M Street
PUBLICATIONS

Order Form

Order additional copies of **THE POWERFUL RADIO WORKBOOK** *or* Place an order for ***Creating Powerful Radio,*** A Communicator's Handbook

❑ **Please send ______ copies of THE POWERFUL RADIO WORKBOOK** U.S. **$39.95** *(plus S&H)*

❑ Please send ______ copies of ***Creating Powerful Radio*** U.S. **$24.95** *(plus S&H)*

NAME ____

COMPANY ____

ADDRESS ____

____

CITY ____________________ STATE ____________________

ZIP/ POSTAL CODE ____________________ COUNTRY ____________________

TELEPHONE ____

FAX ____________________ E-MAIL ____________________

Shipping and Handling

U.S.	$5.00 per book (Priority Mail).
Canada and all others	Call for the latest rates (Air Mail).

Payment

All forms of payment must be in U.S. funds. No COD's please. Discounts are available for educational institutions and multiple-copy orders. Call for more information.

❑ Visa ❑ Mastercard ❑ American Express

❑ Check (U.S. only) ❑ Money Order (U.S. Bank)

Card number ____________________ Exp. date __________

Total amount ____

Name as it appears on the card ______________________________

Billing address (Amex only) ______________________________

Signature ____

Fax orders: **+1-615-251-8798**

Phone orders: Toll-free **1-800-248-4242**; Outside the U.S., call **+1-615-251-1525**.

Mail orders: **M Street Publications**
54 Music Square East, Suite 201
Nashville, TN 37203 USA

M Street PUBLICATIONS

Order Form

Order additional copies of **THE POWERFUL RADIO WORKBOOK** *or* Place an order for ***Creating Powerful Radio,*** A Communicator's Handbook

❑ **Please send _______ copies of THE POWERFUL RADIO WORKBOOK** U.S. **$39.95** *(plus S&H)*

❑ Please send _______ copies of ***Creating Powerful Radio*** U.S. **$24.95** *(plus S&H)*

NAME ____________________

COMPANY ____________________

ADDRESS ____________________

____

CITY ____________________ STATE ____________________

ZIP/ POSTAL CODE ____________________ COUNTRY ____________________

TELEPHONE ____________________

FAX ____________________ E-MAIL ____________________

Shipping and Handling

U.S.	$5.00 per book (Priority Mail).
Canada and all others	Call for the latest rates (Air Mail).

Payment

All forms of payment must be in U.S. funds. No COD's please. Discounts are available for educational institutions and multiple-copy orders. Call for more information.

❑ Visa ❑ Mastercard ❑ American Express

❑ Check (U.S. only) ❑ Money Order (U.S. Bank)

Card number ____________________ Exp. date ____________________

Total amount ____________________

Name as it appears on the card ____________________

Billing address (Amex only) ____________________

Signature ____________________

Fax orders:	**+1-615-251-8798**
Phone orders:	Toll-free **1-800-248-4242**; Outside the U.S., call +**1-615-251-1525**.
Mail orders:	**M Street Publications** **54 Music Square East, Suite 201** **Nashville, TN 37203 USA**

M Street PUBLICATIONS